MAKING FLOWERS

IN PAPER, FABRIC AND RIBBON

MAKING FLOWERS

IN PAPER, FABRIC AND RIBBON

ILLUSTRATIONS BY
MEGUMI BIDDLE

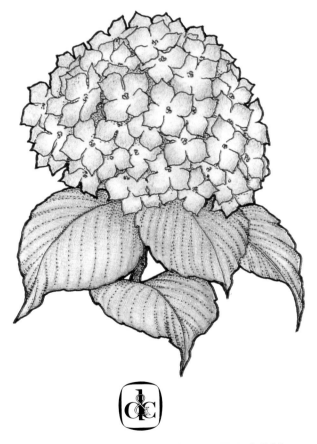

A DAVID & CHARLES CRAFT BOOK

To My Mother, Tomiko Kodama,
for her generosity and encouragement,
My everlasting thanks.

Megumi Biddle

We would like to express our thanks to Neal
Street East for the loan of the many flower
containers, to Paul Biddle for his photography
and to John Cunliffe for his work on the index.

First published 1991
This edition published 1999

Text and illustrations copyright © Steve &
Megumi Biddle 1991, 1999

The right of Steve & Megumi Biddle to be
identified as authors of this work has been
asserted by him/her in accordance with the
Copyright, Designs and Patents Act 1988.

British Library Cataloguing in Publication Data
Biddle, Steve
  Making flowers: in paper, fabric and ribbon.
  1. Artificial flowers. Making
  I. Title II. Biddle, Megumi
  745.5943

  ISBN 0-7153-0985-4

Typeset by Typesetters (Birmingham) Ltd,
Smethwick, West Midlands
and printed in Italy
by L.E.G.O. SpA
for David & Charles plc
Brunel House Newton Abbot Devon

CONTENTS

Introduction 6
General Materials and Techniques 8
SNOWDROP 22
DAFFODIL 26
CHERRY BLOSSOM 30
CANTERBURY BELL AND 34
  FORSYTHIA
TULIP 40
FREESIA 44
CARNATION 48
BIRD OF PARADISE AND 52
  EUCALYPTUS
IRIS 58
HYDRANGEA 62
FOXGLOVE 66
CLEMATIS 70
STRAWBERRY 75
SALVIA 80
PETUNIA 84

FRANGIPANI 89
LILY 94
BOUVARDIA 99
GLADIOLUS 103
POPPY 108
COSMOS 112
NERINE 116
CAMELLIA 120
CYCLAMEN 124
ROSE 128
PEONY 133
Dyeing and Sizing 140
Tips on Petal Cutting 145
Assembling a Bridal Bouquet 149
  and Corsage
Arranging Handmade Flowers 152
Glossary of Tools and Equipment 155
Index 159

INTRODUCTION

Only a little imagination and a few simple techniques are required to capture the fleeting scent of a flower and the beauty of a curved petal. This is what *Making Flowers* is all about.

As paper and fabric are some of the cheapest materials available many of the projects in this book can be started with the minimum of outlay. Each project introduces a new technique, so that by the time you have worked through the book, you will have learned all the skills involved in flower making.

Before you choose which flower to make, we suggest that you read General Materials and Techniques and the Glossary of Tools and Equipment, as these sections cover many of the techniques and tools needed.

Materials mentioned by name are recommended from personal experience. There are, however, many other, equally effective, products available (which may differ by trade name). If you would like further details concerning flower making materials, especially handmade paper, please write to us care of David & Charles.

A final word concerning materials: we have found materials required for flower making in the most unlikely places, ranging from cake decoration suppliers to fashion shops. So be persistent and search around carefully.

In flower making it is the finishing touches and personal style that will make your work look professional. By all means aim to copy the flowers exactly as they appear in the photographs, but do remember that no two artists are alike. What is important is your own personal touch – the feelings and life that you inject into your work. These intangible qualities will allow the flowers to 'speak for themselves'.

We do hope that *Making Flowers* will introduce you to a craft of absorbing interest and that you will develop many creative skills and the confidence to experiment. The flowers in this book have given us many pleasurable hours and we are certain that they will do the same for you.

PARTS OF A FLOWER

You need to take a good close look at real flowers for ideas and an understanding of how they are made. The illustrations in this book contain a lot of detail and give all the necessary information to make the flowers illustrated, but if you want to make your own templates for other flowers, then it is important to have a little understanding of the many different parts of a real flower and how they relate to each other.

PETALS
The petals are brightly coloured to attract the attention of pollen-carrying insects. They are the showpiece of the flower, so make them as beautiful as possible.

CALYX
The calyx is to be found at the junction where the petals are joined to the stem. The calyx is made up of green leaves which keep the flower safe during the bud period. When the flower has blossomed out they can become a decorative element.

STAMENS
The male part of the flower, which makes the grains of pollen. Their tips are often covered in powder.

PISTILS
The female part of the flower, usually found in its centre. Sometimes it is hard to tell the difference between stamens and pistils.

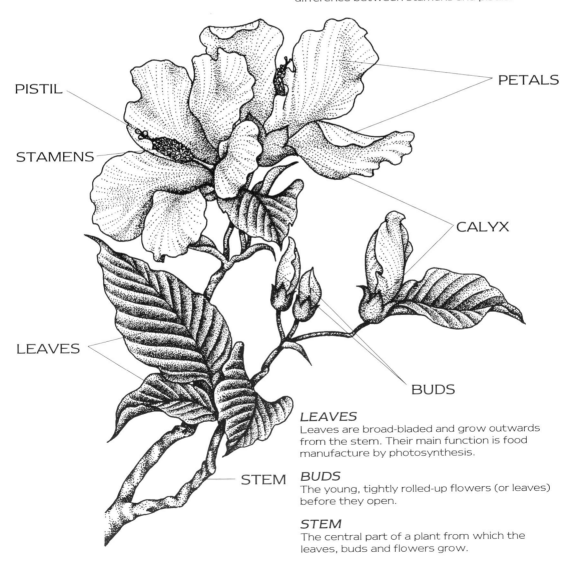

LEAVES
Leaves are broad-bladed and grow outwards from the stem. Their main function is food manufacture by photosynthesis.

BUDS
The young, tightly rolled-up flowers (or leaves) before they open.

STEM
The central part of a plant from which the leaves, buds and flowers grow.

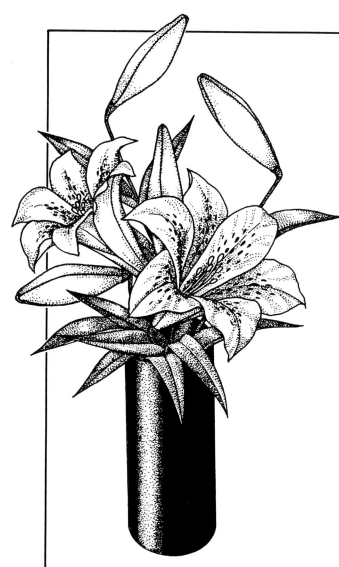

General Materials and Techniques

GENERAL MATERIALS

Before you start it is recommended that you read this section, and the more detailed sections starting on page 140, thoroughly. They describe the many materials, techniques and skills that recur in the instructions.

HANDMADE PAPER

This type of paper can be obtained from Japanese import shops and most of the larger art and craft stores. It is available in a large variety of beautiful colours and textures. Handmade paper can be used to make most types of flowers, as it helps to give the finished result a lovely textural appearance. Also, like other materials, it can be dyed. Do not be concerned if you are unable to obtain handmade paper, as it is possible to substitute any of the other materials.

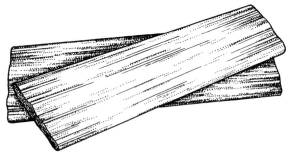

CREPE PAPER

This type of paper can be obtained from stationers, art and craft stores or hobby material suppliers. It is available in white and a large variety of beautiful colours. Crepe paper can be made more interesting in colour and finished texture by a very simple dyeing technique. Its texture is ideal for making bell-shaped flowers or those whose petals have a frill.

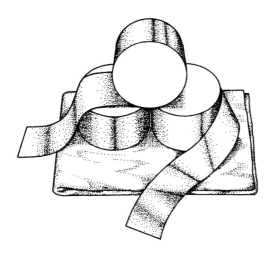

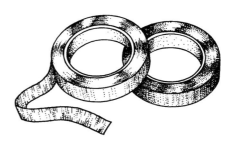

FABRIC AND RIBBON

Cotton, satin, poplin, velvet and silk are ideal fabrics for flower making. Maybe you already have some pieces of fabric left over from dressmaking. Ribbon can be obtained from haberdashery stores. It is available in a large variety of textures and colours. Also, like crepe paper, fabric and ribbon can be made more interesting in colour by very simple dyeing techniques. Before starting to cut out any templates make sure that your fabrics have been sized (this does not apply to velvet).

FLORAL TAPE

Floral tape (stem tape/florists' tape/gutta tape) can be obtained from florists, art and craft stores and hobby material suppliers. It is available in a large range of colours. If you cannot obtain floral tape in a specified colour, it can be dyed. Do not buy the shiny plastic floral tape that is used for fresh flowers, as its plastic coating makes it unsuitable for taping together the various parts of a handmade flower.

STAMENS

These can be obtained from haberdashery stores, art and craft stores, hobby material suppliers and cake decoration suppliers. They are available in a large variety of colours and sizes. Stamens are usually supplied as double-headed strings, which then can be cut or folded in half as required. If you cannot obtain stamens in a specified colour, it is possible to dye them.

WIRE

This can be obtained from florists, hardware stores, art and craft stores, hobby material suppliers and cake decoration suppliers. It is available in a large range of gauges and pre-cut lengths and can be obtained either uncovered or covered with paper of a particular colour (usually green or white).

Note: Both metric and imperial measurements have been given throughout. They are not exact equivalents, so follow one system or the other exclusively – do not mix the two systems.

GENERAL TECHNIQUES

MAKING A TEMPLATE

A template is employed to transfer the illustrated pattern from the page onto your material. When transferring the pattern onto crepe paper make sure that its grain runs in the direction of the pattern's double-headed arrow. In the case of fabric or ribbon make sure that the double-headed arrow is pointing along the bias (a line diagonal to the grain of the fabric or ribbon). This does not apply to Japanese handmade paper, which has no grain.

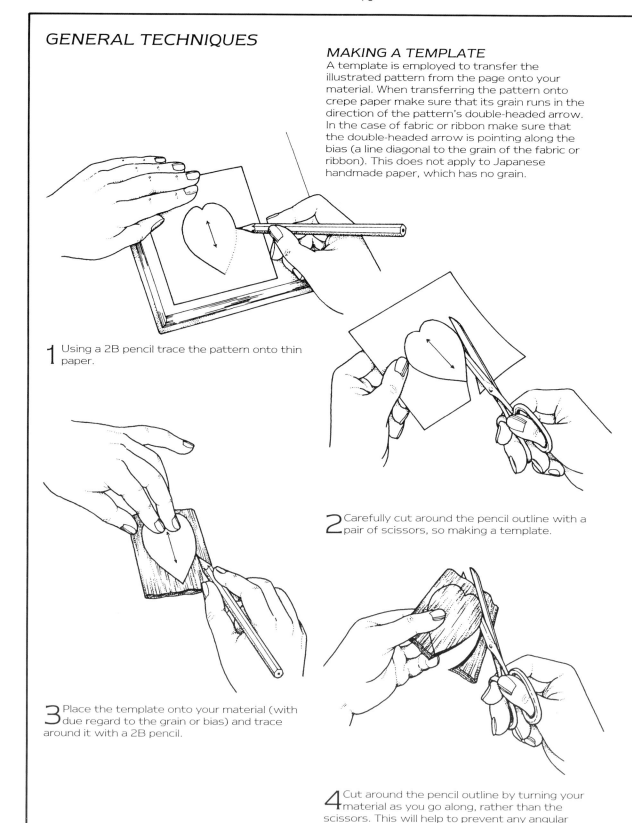

1 Using a 2B pencil trace the pattern onto thin paper.

2 Carefully cut around the pencil outline with a pair of scissors, so making a template.

3 Place the template onto your material (with due regard to the grain or bias) and trace around it with a 2B pencil.

4 Cut around the pencil outline by turning your material as you go along, rather than the scissors. This will help to prevent any angular irregularities in the finished shape. As all the illustrated patterns in this book are life-size there is no need to reduce or enlarge them.

LEAF EMBOSSING
Leaves come in many different shapes and sizes, each with its particular vein pattern. To make your leaves look realistic always use this very simple technique.

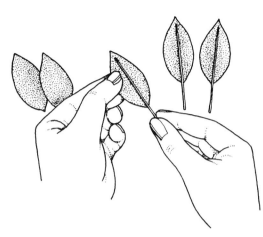

1 Stopping just short of the leaf's tip, place a little glue along its spine with the aid of a cocktail stick.

2 Glue a length of wire onto the leaf (usually the wire will protrude past the leaf's bottom point). Make sure that the wire is firmly glued into place before progressing to the next step.

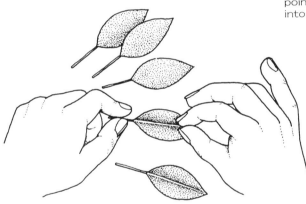

3 Turn the leaf over (so that the wired side is facing downwards) and score along its spine with your thumb and fingernails, so making a raised impression of the wire.

4 Place a few folded tissues onto a soft, but springy surface (like the top of the ironing board or your lap) and put the leaf (wired side facing downwards) on top. Using a spatula or a teaspoon handle, score on the leaf's veins.

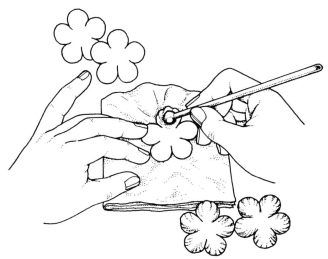

CUPPING

There are many ways to give form and shape that will add that extra touch of realism to a handmade flower. The final choice of material will usually govern the technique. Cupping works best with crepe paper or handmade paper.

Place a few folded tissues onto a soft, but springy surface (like the top of the ironing board or your lap) and put the petal on top. Using a round-headed tool (the head of a knitting needle or the bowl of a teaspoon) press down and round and round from the tip of each petal towards its centre, so making the petal cup-like in appearance.

HEATING

This technique works best with fabric or ribbon. Before you start make sure that you have completed any required preparations like dyeing and sizing.

There is available an electric iron especially developed for flower making. By fixing special heads to the iron, it is possible to add softness and texture to the petals and leaves.

If you have such an iron then by all means use it, but if you do not have one, use a heated teaspoon. Heat the teaspoon in boiling water for a few minutes, quickly dry it and carefully follow the cupping technique. You may have to reheat the teaspoon several times to achieve the required result.

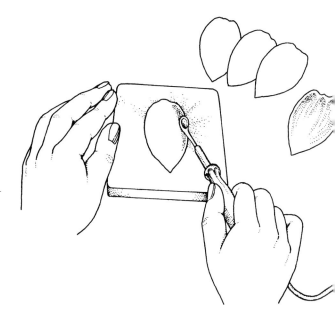

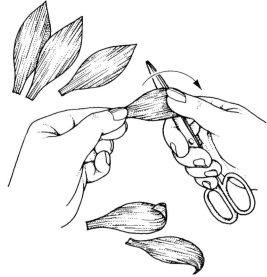

CURLING

This technique works best with crepe paper.

Place one edge of the crepe paper (along the direction of its grain) between your thumb and the closed blades of a pair of scissors. Draw the blades firmly across the crepe paper, so curling it in the process. The strength of the finished curl depends upon how firmly the closed blades are drawn across the crepe paper.

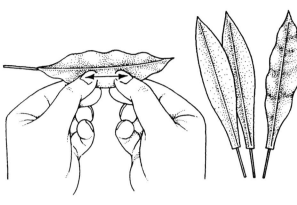

FLUTING

The following four stretch techniques use the bias or grain of the material to give the petals a feeling of form and softness.

For fluting, hold the petal's edge between your thumbs and forefingers as shown and gently pull it in opposite directions. Continue fluting all the way around the petal's edge.

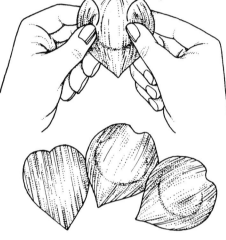

STRETCH CUPPING

Hold the petal's middle between your thumbs and forefingers and gently push and stretch it outwards in opposite directions.

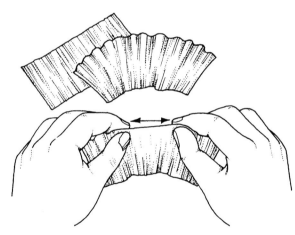

FRILLING

Hold the petal's edge between your thumbs and forefingers as shown and gently stretch it in opposite directions. Continue frilling all the way around the required length of the petal.

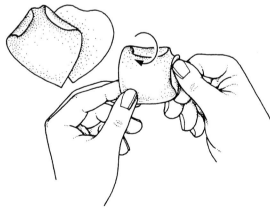

ROSE CURLING

To give a soft curl to a petal, especially that of a rose, gently roll its upper edges over between your thumb and forefinger.

CRINKLING

Many flowers, like the iris and gladiolus, have a lovely crinkled texture to their petals. This effect is very easily obtained using a damp cloth, though the technique only works for handmade paper and fabric. It is very easy to learn, but you will need to practise a little on a piece of spare material.

Before you start, dampen a large cotton handkerchief. Squeeze out any excess water, so that the handkerchief just feels moist. If the handkerchief is too wet the crinkling will not take place and you will end up with a soggy lump of material. Secondly, make sure that any leaf or petal wires are firmly glued into place and that the glue is dry, and ensure that the wired side is facing upwards.

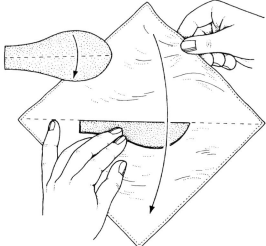

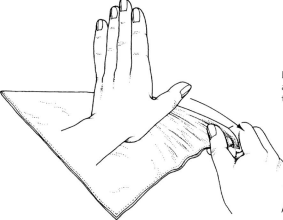

1 Place the handkerchief before you, so that it looks like a diamond. Fold the petal in half lengthways. Place the folded petal centrally along the handkerchief's horizontal length. Fold the handkerchief in half from top to bottom.

2 Place the heel of one hand firmly on top of the petal. With your working hand hold one top corner of the handkerchief and pull it sideways, so stretching the handkerchief's bias. Making sure that you maintain a firm pressure on the petal, keep on pulling the handkerchief and at the same time swing the handkerchief down towards you . . .

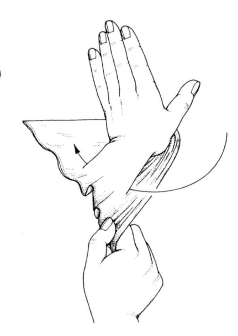

3 . . . so passing it underneath your other hand.

4 Gently unfold the handkerchief and inside its folds you will find the crinkled petal. Keeping the petal's cup-like shape, gently open it out and place it in a safe place to dry.

In step 2 it does not matter if you are right or left-handed, as long as you have the petal's tip pointing towards your working hand when you are pulling the handkerchief.

SINGLE WIRING

30 gauge wire is used to gather and fasten together petals. When making flowers that have petals joined together in one piece, like a freesia, it is best to wire them together singly.

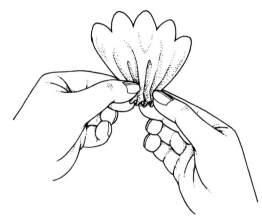

1 Hold the petal between your thumbs and forefingers. Make small, even gathers in the petal's bottom edge, making it fan-like in appearance.

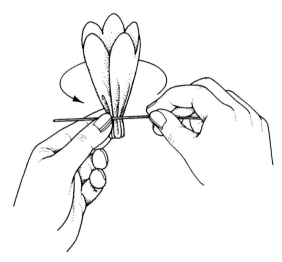

2 Being careful not to let go of the gathers, gently wrap the petal's sides around, so that they overlap slightly. Starting about 1cm (½in) up from the petal's bottom edge bind a short length of 30 gauge wire firmly around the gathers . . .

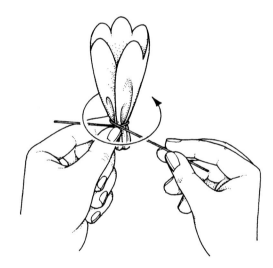

3 . . . two or three times.

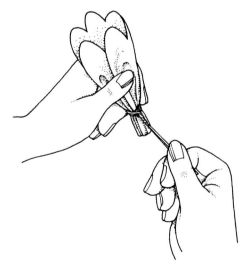

4 Hold the petal in one hand and tightly twist the two ends of wire together with the other, so preventing the wire from coming undone and the petal from falling apart. Do not cut off any excess wire, as it will be needed to fasten the petal onto the stem.

GROUP WIRING

When making flowers that have a great number of petals, like a rose, it is best to fasten them together in a group.

Before you start, bend a long length of 30 gauge wire in half.

1 Between your thumbs and forefingers make small, even gathers in the bottom of the petal, so making it cup-like in appearance.

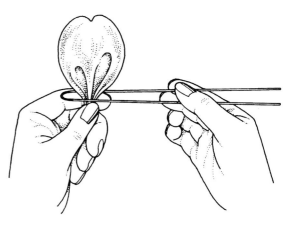

2 Making sure that the petal's cupped side is facing upwards, insert it into the bent end of the wire. Try to have about 1cm (½in) of the petal's bottom point protruding below the wire.

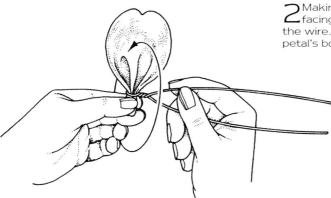

3 Hold the two ends of the bent wire and turn the petal over, two or three times, so twisting the two ends and at the same time fastening the petal between them.

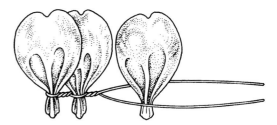

4 Making sure that it overlaps and is as near as possible to the previous one, repeat steps 1 and 2 with another petal. Repeat step 3, being careful when the petal is turned over that it is held together with the previous petal(s).

Repeat steps 1 to 4 as many times as necessary. Do not cut off any excess wire, as it will be needed to fasten the petals onto the stem.

FLOWER CENTRE

The flower centre is made up of stamens and pistils. They are a very important part of the finished flower as they help to give it a personality.

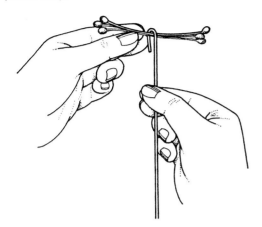

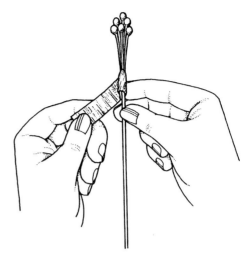

1 Bend a small hook into one end of a length of wire. Place the hook over the middle of the required number of stamens. Bend the stamens upwards.

2 Neatly tape around the stems of the stamens, about 0.5cm (¼in) up from the hook, so fastening them onto the hooked wire.

BUILDING UP A FLOWER

Even though many of the flowers in this book are different in appearance, the basic steps for building them up are broadly as follows.

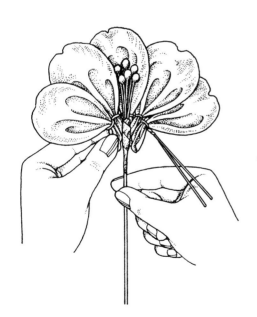

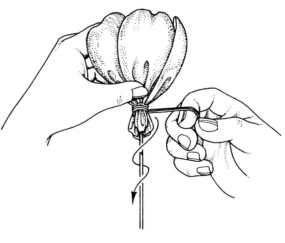

1 Making sure that the wire which fastens the petals together lies just above the point where the stamens meet the tape, wrap the petals around the flower centre.

2 Firmly bind the excess wire around the base of the petals, so fastening them onto the stem. If possible, twist the remaining wire around the stem. (In flower making, the space between the petal's bottom edge and the binding is called the *base*. It is often used as a working area for binding, gluing and taping.)

(continued overleaf) 17

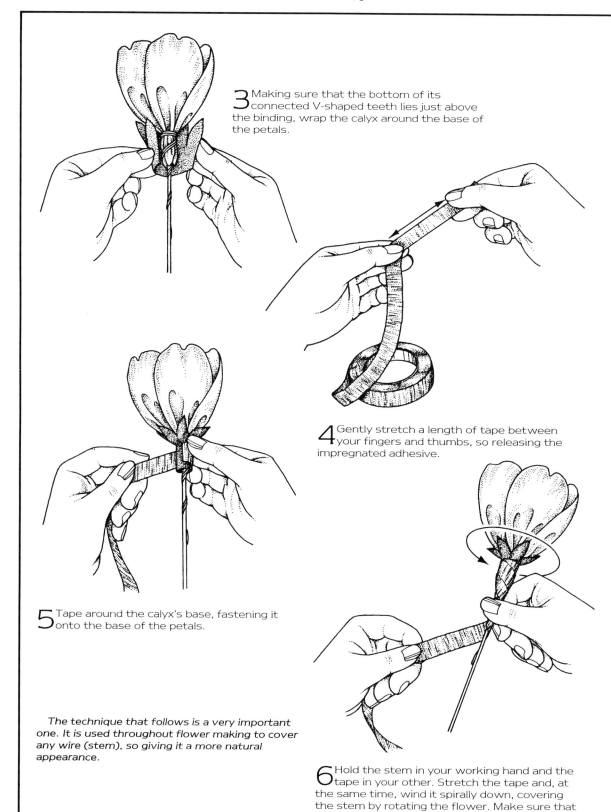

3 Making sure that the bottom of its connected V-shaped teeth lies just above the binding, wrap the calyx around the base of the petals.

4 Gently stretch a length of tape between your fingers and thumbs, so releasing the impregnated adhesive.

5 Tape around the calyx's base, fastening it onto the base of the petals.

The technique that follows is a very important one. It is used throughout flower making to cover any wire (stem), so giving it a more natural appearance.

6 Hold the stem in your working hand and the tape in your other. Stretch the tape and, at the same time, wind it spirally down, covering the stem by rotating the flower. Make sure that you allow the edges of each coil to overlap just a little, as this helps to give the stem a neat appearance. This taping gets much easier with practice.

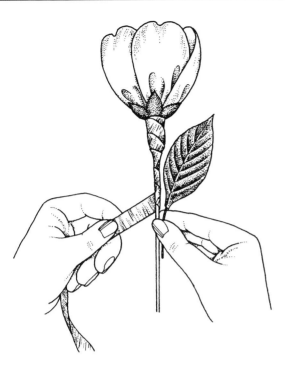

7 At the required point, place a leaf against the stem so that its wired side is facing outwards.

8 Turning the stem and the leaf's protruding wire together as one, tape the leaf into place by repeating step 6, so covering the protruding wire. For a neater result, try to take in just a tiny fraction of the leaf's base as you are taping. Continue taping . . .

9 . . . and repeat steps 7 and 8 to add on buds, extra leaves and flowers. For a professional result always make sure that you continue taping to the end of the stem.

MAKING A BUD

The same basic steps are used for all buds.

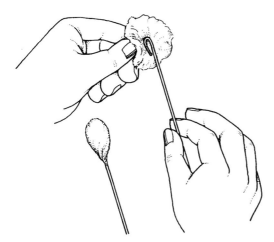

1 Bend a small hook into one end of the required length of wire. Little by little, wrap small amounts of cotton wool around the hook, so making a pompon. The actual shape and size of the pompon is always mentioned in the text.

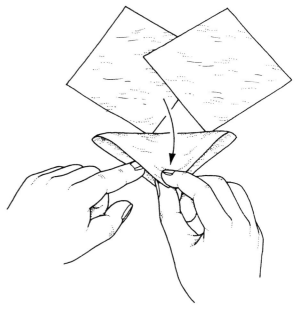

2 Place the bud material before you like a diamond and fold it in half from top to bottom.

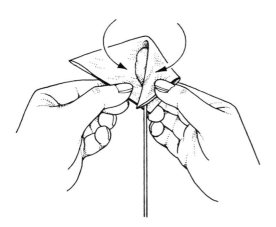

3 Being careful that no cotton wool shows, wrap the bud around the pompon and . . .

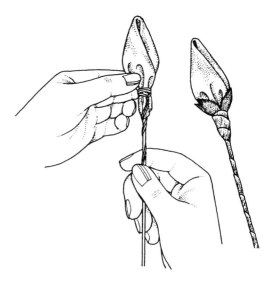

4 . . . bind it on to the wire with a small length of 30 gauge wire (or tape). Twist any excess wire around the stem. Add on, and tape into place around the bud's base any calyx that is required. Continue taping to the end of the stem.

FINISHING TOUCHES

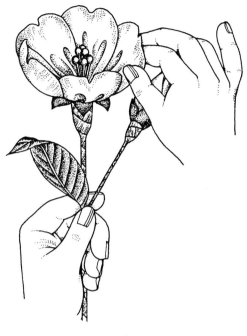

1 For ease of making, almost every flower is in a 'closed' position. It is important, therefore, that you give 'life' to a flower by opening out the petals and leaves (hiding their wired side) and arranging the angle of the stem and flower. You can arrange a flower to suit your own personal taste or you can try to reproduce Mother Nature.

2 The length of the stem and how far you cover it in tape all depend upon your personal taste and flower making experience. For example, if you are making flowers for a corsage, then cut their stems as short as possible.

3 If you plan to arrange your flowers in a vase, make their stems longer than they should be, so that later on you can cut them to the required length.

Do try to save yourself a lot of time, expense and unnecessary waste of materials by bearing in mind the main purpose of the flowers you wish to make and then planning your work accordingly.

SNOWDROP

This is a good flower to make in winter, as the green, strap-shaped leaves and nodding white flowers will herald the arrival of spring.

Green handmade paper or fabric
White crepe paper
Green floral tape
20 and 24 gauge green covered wires
1 white stamen
Light-green felt-tip pen
PVA glue
Tools (scissors, ruler etc)

For one snowdrop cut the following:

Part	Material	Quantity	Colour
Petal A	crepe paper	3	white
Petal B	crepe paper	1	white
Leaves L/M/S	handmade paper or fabric	1 of each	green
Calyx	handmade paper or fabric	1	green

The illustrated patterns are life-size. Trace them onto paper and use these templates to mark out the above parts of the flower. All techniques used here are fully described in General Materials and Techniques.

LEAVES

PETAL A

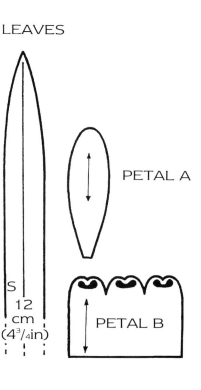

L
18 cm
(7in)

M
15 cm
(6in)

S
12 cm
(4³/₄in)

PETAL B

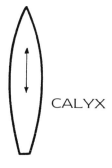

CALYX

SNOWDROP

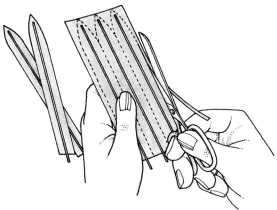

LEAVES

1 Cut three 18cm (7in) lengths of 24 gauge wire. Leaving a space of about 1.2cm (½in) between each length of wire, glue them onto the green material.

2 When the lengths of wire are firmly glued into place, cut out leaves L, M and S.

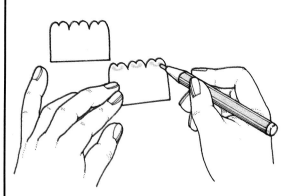

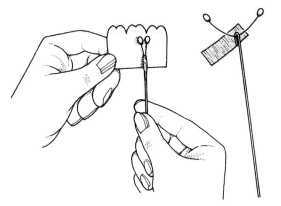

FLOWER

3 As per the illustrated pattern, colour the tips of petal B with the light-green felt-tip pen.

4 Make one flower centre consisting of a 20cm (8in) length of 20 gauge wire, the white stamen and a length of tape. With its coloured tips on the outside, wrap petal B around the flower centre, so that its sides overlap slightly.

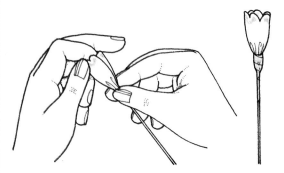

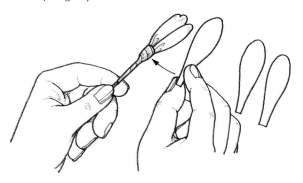

5 Hold the flower centre and petal B together between your thumb and forefinger. Gently open out petal B, so making it bell-like in appearance. Tape around petal B's base, so fastening it onto the stem.

6 With the aid of a little glue, place petals A around petal B's base.

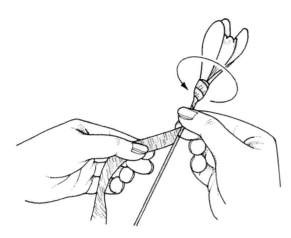

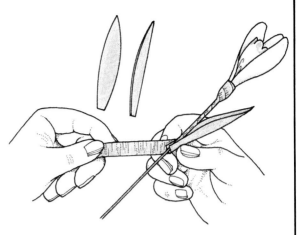

7 Tape around the base of the petals, so fastening them onto the stem. Continue taping along the stem to a length of about 3cm (1¼in).

8 To join together – fold the calyx in half lengthways. About 2cm (¾in) below the flower's base tape the calyx, at its base, around the stem. Continue taping to the end of the stem.

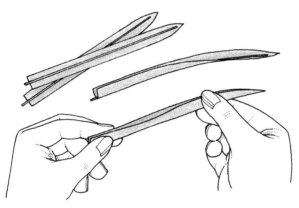

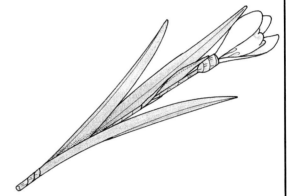

9 With their wires on the inside, fold the leaves in half lengthways.

10 Making sure that they are not any taller than the flower, tape the leaves, at their bases, around the stem. Continue taping to the end of the stem.

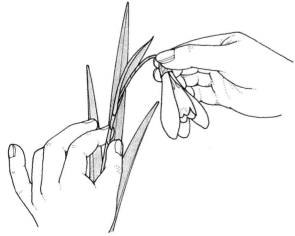

11 Finishing off – gently bend the stem over a little, to make the snowdrop look lifelike.

12 Make a few more snowdrops and, using dry gravel, arrange them together in a flowerpot.

DAFFODIL

The daffodil, with its six star-like petals and golden flower, will give a spring feeling to any arrangement.

Green handmade paper or fabric
White and yellow crepe papers
Green floral tape
20 gauge green covered wire
30 gauge wire
PVA glue
Tools (scissors, ruler etc)

For one daffodil cut the following:

Part	Material	Quantity	Colour
Petal	crepe paper	1	yellow or white
Leaves	handmade paper		
L/S	or fabric	1 of each	green
Calyx	handmade paper		
	or fabric	1	green
Trumpet	crepe paper	1	yellow

The illustrated patterns are life-size. Trace them onto paper and use these templates to mark out the above parts of the flower. All techniques used here are fully described in General Materials and Techniques.

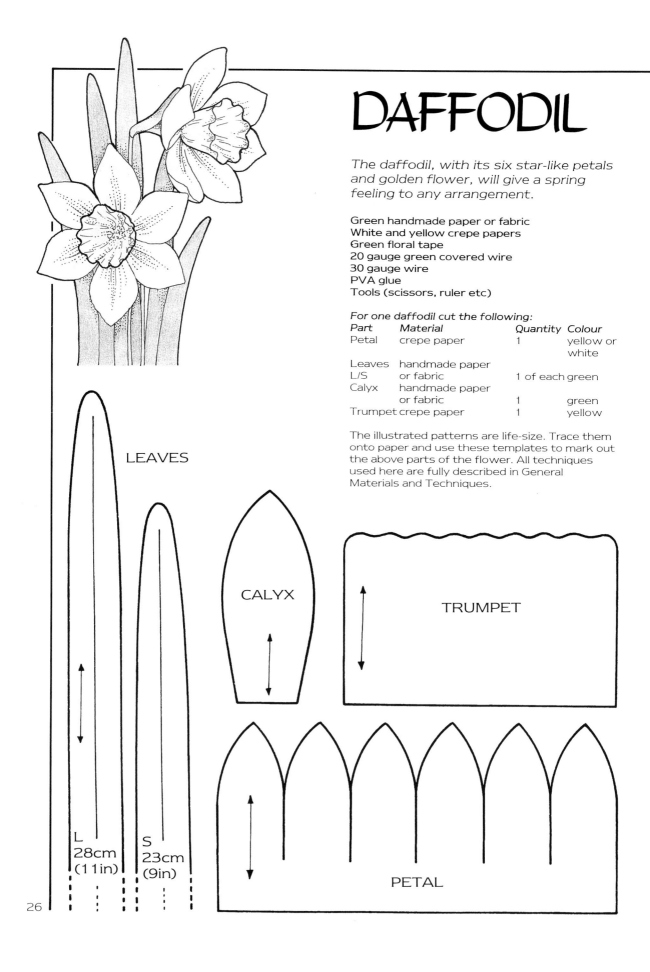

LEAVES

CALYX

TRUMPET

L
28cm
(11in)

S
23cm
(9in)

PETAL

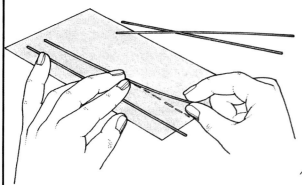

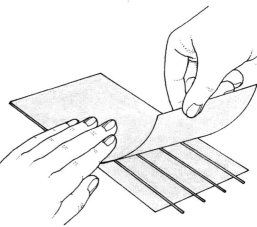

LEAVES

1 Cut two 28cm (11in) lengths of 20 gauge wire. Leaving a space of about 1.4cm (½in) between each length of wire, glue them onto the green material.

2 Glue another piece of green material on top of the lengths of wire.

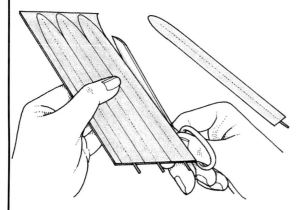

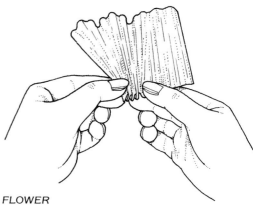

3 When the lengths of wire are firmly glued into place, cut out leaves L and S. If you are planning to make a lot of daffodils it is easier to mass produce their leaves this way than to make them individually.

FLOWER

4 Make small, even gathers along the trumpet's bottom edge, making it fan-like.

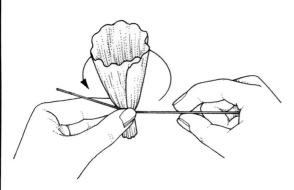

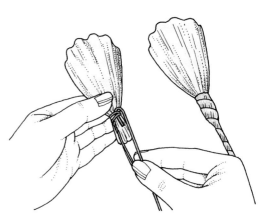

5 Being careful not to let go of the gathers, wrap the trumpet around on itself, so that its sides overlap slightly. Firmly bind a short length of 30 gauge wire around the trumpet's base, starting about 1cm (½in) up from the trumpet's bottom edge.

6 Cut a fairly long length of 20 gauge wire and bend a small hook into one end. Hook the wire into the binding. Tape around the binding, hiding it and, at the same time, fastening the trumpet onto the hooked wire.

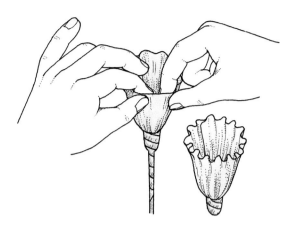

7 Frill the trumpet's top edge.

8 Make small, even gathers along the petal's bottom edge, making it fan-like in appearance.

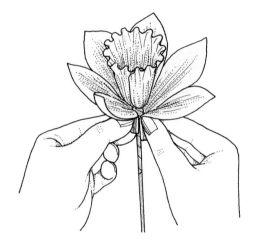

9 Wrap the petal around the trumpet's base.

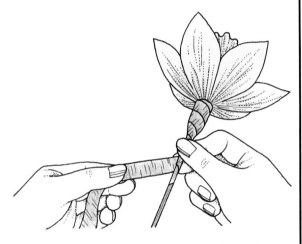

10 Tape around the petal's base, fastening it onto the stem. Continue taping along the stem to a length of about 3cm (1¼in).

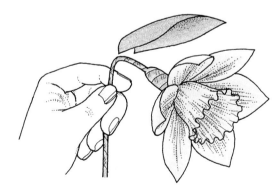

TO JOIN TOGETHER

11 About 2cm (¾in) below the flower's base gently bend the stem over, so that it becomes daffodil-like in appearance. Tape the calyx, at its base, around the bend in the stem. Continue taping to the end of the stem.

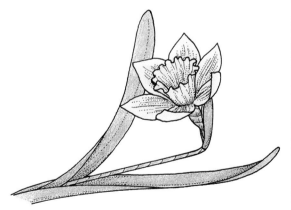

12 Making sure that they are not any taller than the flower, tape the leaves, at their bases, around the stem. Continue taping to the end of the stem.

CHERRY BLOSSOM

Cherry blossom has a very short life span and it can be swept away by any sudden breezes. One way to retain the 'fleeting moment' of the cherry blossom is of course to make your own.

Brown, cherry-pink and olive-green handmade papers or fabrics
Brown and olive-green floral tapes
18 gauge wire
24 gauge green covered wire
16 yellow stamens
Cotton wool
PVA glue
Tools (scissors, ruler etc)

For one branch of cherry blossom cut the following:

Part	Material	Quantity	Colour
Petal	handmade paper or fabric	16	cherry pink
Leaf L	handmade paper or fabric	2	brown
Leaf S	handmade paper or fabric	2	olive green
Bud	handmade paper or fabric	8	cherry pink
Calyx A	handmade paper or fabric	4	olive green
Calyx B	handmade paper or fabric	8	olive green

The illustrated patterns are life-size. Trace them onto paper and use these templates to mark out the above parts of the flower. All techniques used here are fully described in General Materials and Techniques.

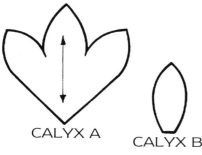

CALYX A   CALYX B

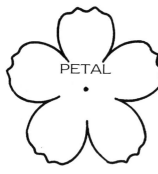

PETAL

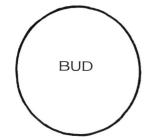

BUD

LEAF S

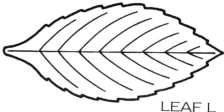

LEAF L

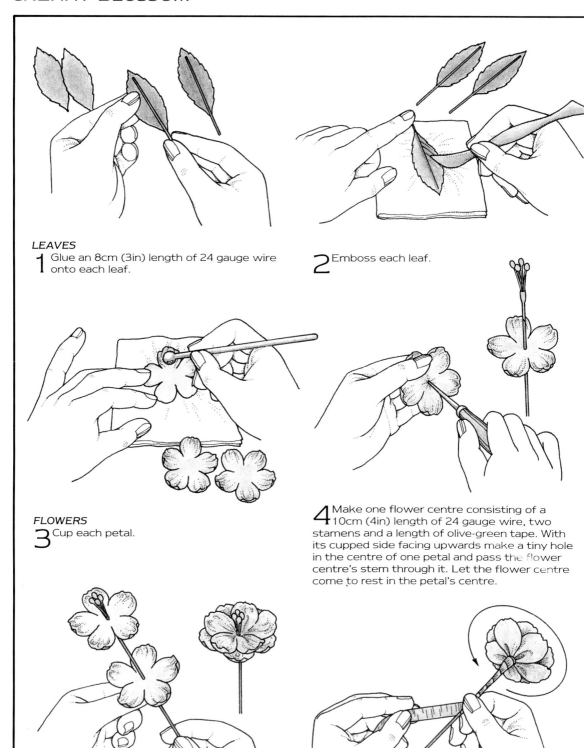

LEAVES

1 Glue an 8cm (3in) length of 24 gauge wire onto each leaf.

2 Emboss each leaf.

FLOWERS

3 Cup each petal.

4 Make one flower centre consisting of a 10cm (4in) length of 24 gauge wire, two stamens and a length of olive-green tape. With its cupped side facing upwards make a tiny hole in the centre of one petal and pass the flower centre's stem through it. Let the flower centre come to rest in the petal's centre.

5 Make a tiny hole in the centre of another petal. Carefully position this petal underneath the previous one. With a little glue fix the petals together and, at the same time, pinch their centres from underneath.

6 Fasten the petals, at their bases, onto the stem with olive-green tape. Repeat steps 4 to 6 with the remaining stamens and petals.

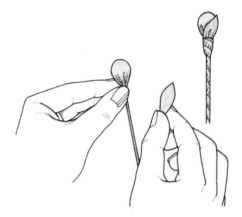

BUDS

7 Make one little fingertip-sized pompon consisting of a 10cm (4in) length of 24 gauge wire and a little cotton wool. Completely cover the pompon with a bud.

8 Glue one calyx B onto the bud's base. Tape around their bases, so fastening them onto the stem. Continue taping to the end of the stem. Repeat steps 7 and 8 with the remaining buds. The end result of this patient work should be eight flowers and eight buds.

TO JOIN TOGETHER

9 Making sure that they are not of the same height, tape two leaves S, two buds and one flower together into a group.

10 At the joint where all the stems meet, tape on one calyx A. Continue taping to the end of the stem.

11 Make three more groups, one consisting of three flowers, two buds and one calyx A. The other two each consisting of one leaf L, two buds, two flowers and one calyx A.

12 With the brown tape fasten the four groups onto a long length of 18 gauge wire, to form a branch-like arrangement.

CANTERBURY BELL AND FORSYTHIA

When arranged together the large, showy flowers of the Canterbury bell and the dainty yellow blooms of the forsythia will help to lighten any dark corner.

Green handmade paper or fabric
Purple and yellow crepe papers
Brown and green floral tapes
20 and 24 gauge green covered wires
30 gauge wire
19 yellow stamens (14 for the Canterbury bell
   and 5 for the forsythia)
Tools (scissors, ruler etc)

For one grouping of Canterbury bell flowers cut the following:

Part	Material	Quantity	Colour
Petals			
L/S	crepe paper	2 of each	purple
Leaf	handmade paper or fabric	4	green
Bud	crepe paper	2	purple
Calyx	handmade paper or fabric	6	green

The illustrated patterns are life-size. Trace them onto paper and use these templates to mark out the above parts of the flowers. All techniques used here are fully described in General Materials and Techniques. The illustrated patterns for the forsythia's petals and bud can be found on page 38.

BUD

CALYX

PETAL S

PETAL L

LEAF

CANTERBURY BELL

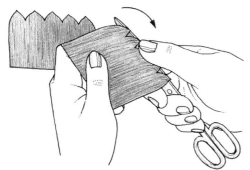

FLOWER

1 Curl the tips of petals L and S.

2 Make small, even gathers along one petal's bottom edge, making it fan-like.

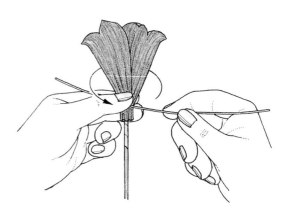

3 Make one flower centre consisting of an 8cm (3in) length of 24 gauge wire, three stamens and a length of tape. Making sure that the petal's tips are curling outwards, place the flower centre onto it. Wrap the petal around the flower centre, so that its sides overlap slightly.

4 Firmly bind a short length of 30 gauge wire around the petal's base, starting about 1cm (½in) up from the petal's bottom edge, fastening it onto the stem.

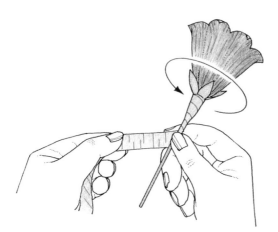

5 Tape one calyx around the flower's base. Continue taping along the stem to a length of about 3cm (1¼in).

6 About 2cm (¾in) below the flower's base, tape one leaf, at its base, around the stem. Continue taping to the end of the stem.

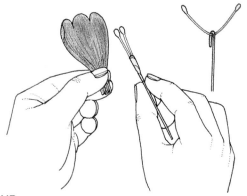

7 Gently open out the flower, making it bell-like. Repeat steps 2 to 7 with the remaining petals.

BUD

8 Make one flower centre consisting of an 8cm (3in) length of 24 gauge wire, one stamen and a length of tape. Repeat steps 1 and 2 with the bud. Making sure that the bud's tips are curling inwards, place the flower centre onto it.

9 Wrap the bud around the flower centre, so that its sides overlap slightly. Wrap one calyx around the bud's base. Tape around their bases, so fastening them onto the stem. Continue taping to the end of the stem. Repeat steps 8 and 9 with the remaining bud. The end result of this patient work should be two small flowers, two large flowers and two buds.

TO JOIN TOGETHER

10 Tape the buds together. Continue taping . . .

11 . . . and add on the flowers, each about 2cm (¾in) apart, making sure that they range from small . . .

12 . . . through to large. Continue taping to the end of the stem. Bend the flowers gently down, to make the Canterbury bell look lifelike.

FORSYTHIA

For one spray of forsythia cut the following:
Petals
L/S   crepe paper   4 of each yellow
Bud   crepe paper   2   yellow

The illustrated patterns are life-size. Trace them onto paper and use these templates to mark out the above parts of the flowers. All techniques used here are fully described in General Materials and Techniques.

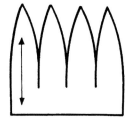

PETAL S

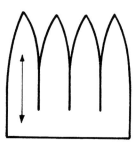

PETAL L

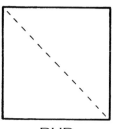

BUD

FORSYTHIA

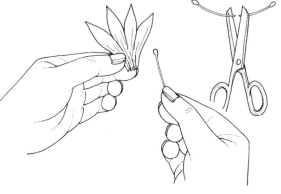

FLOWER

1 Cut four of the stamens in half. Make small, even gathers along one petal's bottom edge, making it fan-like. Place one half stamen onto the petal.

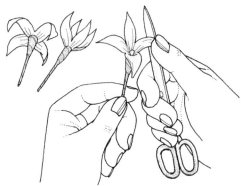
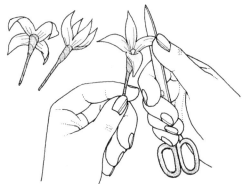

3 Curl the petals of the large flowers outwards and those of the small flowers inwards.

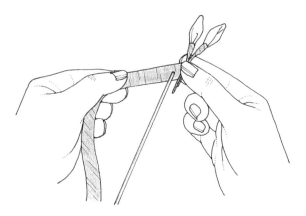

TO JOIN TOGETHER

5 Fasten the two buds onto one end of a length of 20 gauge wire with the brown tape. Continue taping . . .

TULIP
(overleaf)

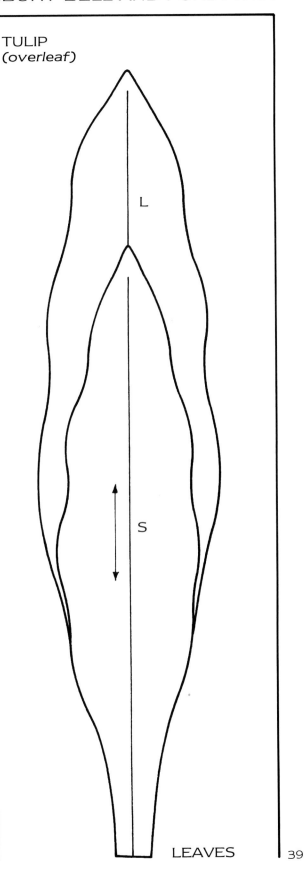

L

S

LEAVES

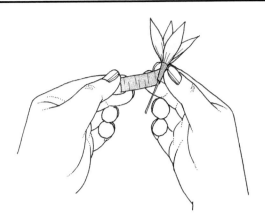

2 Wrap the petal around the half stamen, so that its sides overlap slightly. Fasten the petal and stamen together with green tape. Continue taping to the end of the stamen's stem. Repeat steps 1 and 2 with the remaining petals and half stamens. The end result of this patient work should be four small flowers and four large flowers.

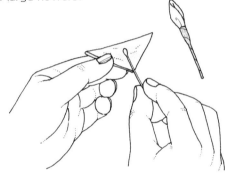

BUD
4 Cut the remaining stamen in half. Make two buds, each one consisting of one half stamen, one bud and a length of tape. Continue taping to the end of each stamen's stem.

6 . . . and add on the flowers, each about 2cm (³⁄₄in) apart, making sure that they range from small through to large. Continue taping to the end of the stem and arrange realistically.

TULIP

The distinctive flower and tall, elegant stem of the tulip will add a certain kind of beauty to any room.

Green, pink, or any other tulip-coloured
    handmade papers or fabrics
Light-green floral tape
20 and 24 gauge green covered wires
A few tissues
Cotton handkerchief
Cotton wool
PVA glue
Tools (scissors, ruler etc)

For one tulip cut the following:

Part	Material	Quantity	Colour
Petals L/S	handmade paper or fabric	3 of each	pink
Leaves L/S	handmade paper or fabric	1 of each	green

The illustrated patterns are life-size. Trace them onto paper and use these templates to mark out the above parts of the flower. All techniques used here are fully described in General Materials and Techniques. The illustrated patterns for the tulip's leaves can be found on page 39.

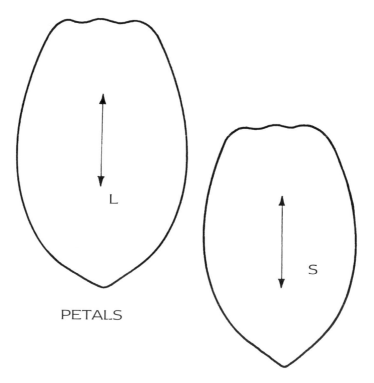

L

S

PETALS

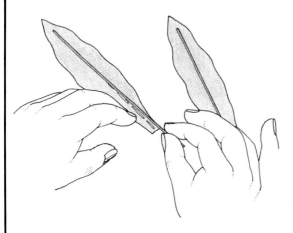

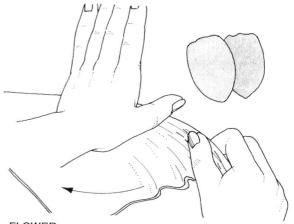

LEAVES

1 From the 24 gauge wire cut two lengths just a little shorter than the lengths of the leaves. Glue the lengths of wire onto their respective leaves.

FLOWER

2 Crinkle each petal.

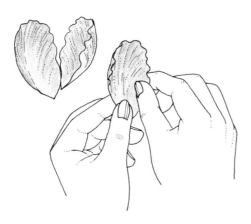

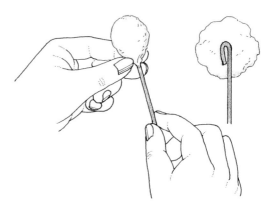

3 Keeping their cup-like shape, gently open out each petal.

4 Make one thumbtip-sized pompon consisting of a 25cm (10in) length of 20 gauge wire and a little cotton wool.

5 Keeping its ball shape, wrap tape around the pompon, and fasten it onto the stem. Continue taping along the stem to a length of about 2cm (¾in).

6 With their cupped side facing inwards glue petals S around the pompon's base, so that they overlap each other and form a tightly closed bud-like shape.

7 Repeat step 6 with petals L, making sure that they are glued in an alternating pattern to petals S.

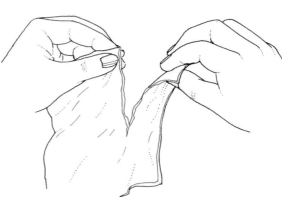

8 Tear up the tissues (along their length) into strips that are about 3cm (1¼in) wide.

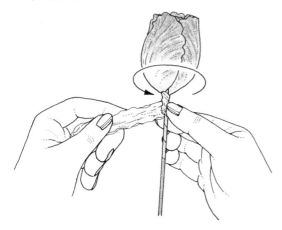

9 To imitate the tulip's fleshy stem, thicken it out by wrapping it with the strips of tissue.

10 Starting adjacent to the flower, neatly cover the tissue with tape. Continue taping to the end of the stem.

11 About 15cm (6in) below the flower's base tape leaf S, at its base, around the stem. Continue taping . . .

12 . . . and, about a further 5cm (2in) down, tape leaf L, at its base, around the stem. Continue taping to the end of the stem. Bend the leaves outwards gently.

FREESIA

The freesia's delicately coloured flowers will bring a simple but charming welcome to any day.

Yellow crepe paper
Light-green floral tape
20 and 24 gauge green covered wires
30 gauge wire
8 white stamens
Orange ink or direct dye
Tools (scissors, ruler etc)

For one stem of freesias cut the following:

Part	Material	Quantity	Colour
Petals XL/L/M/S	crepe paper	1 of each	yellow
Bud	crepe paper	1	yellow

The illustrated patterns are life-size. Trace them onto paper and use these templates to mark out the above parts of the flower. All techniques used here are fully described in General Materials and Techniques/Dyeing and Sizing.

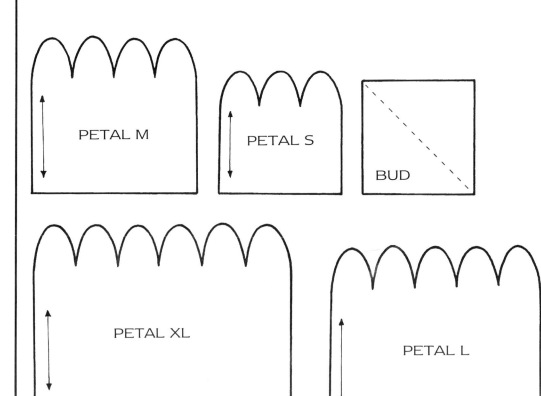

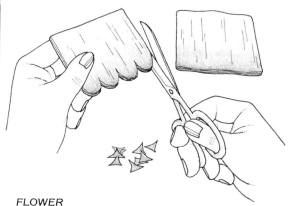

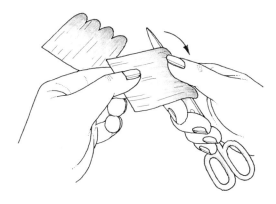

FLOWER

1 Using the dyeing technique for crepe paper dye one end of the crepe paper. The ideal colouring, from top to bottom, should be orange gradually passing through to yellow. (Instead of orange you could use purple or any other freesia-like colour.) Being careful to have the orange area at the top, cut out the petals and bud.

2 Curl the tips of petals XL, L and M outwards and those of petal S inwards.

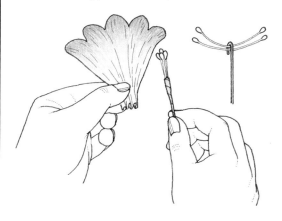

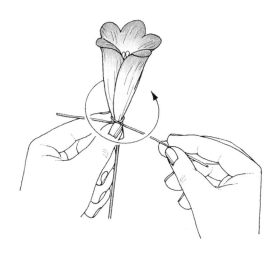

3 Make one flower centre consisting of a 6cm (2¼in) length of 24 gauge wire, two stamens and a length of tape. Make small, even gathers along petal L's bottom edge, so making it fan-like in appearance.

4 Making sure that petal L's tips are curling outwards, place the flower centre onto it. Wrap the petal around the flower centre so that its sides overlap slightly. Firmly bind a short length of 30 gauge wire around the petal's base, starting about 1cm (½in) up from the petal's bottom edge, so fastening it onto the stem.

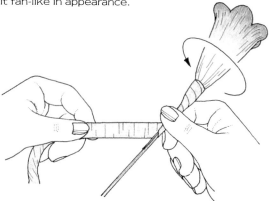

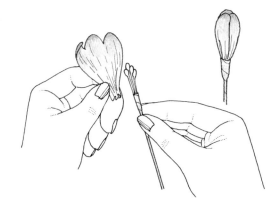

5 Tape around the binding, hiding it. Continue taping to the end of the stem, so making one large flower. Repeat steps 3 to 5 with petals XL, M and S.

6 (When making petal S ensure that the petal's tips are curling inwards when its flower centre is placed onto it.)

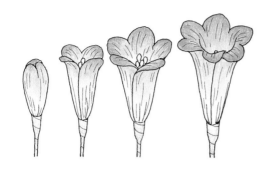

7 You should now have four flowers.

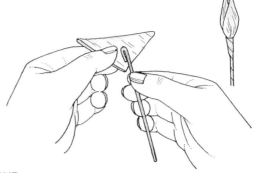

BUD

8 Make one bud consisting of a 6cm (2¼in) length of 24 gauge wire, the bud and a length of tape. Continue taping to the end of the stem.

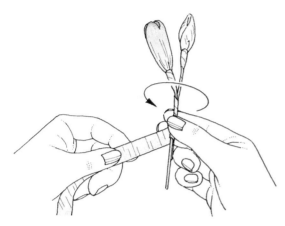

TO JOIN TOGETHER

9 About 2cm (¾in) below the bud's base tape the small flower onto the stem. Continue taping . . .

10 . . . and add on the flowers, each about 2cm (¾in) apart, making sure that they range from medium . . .

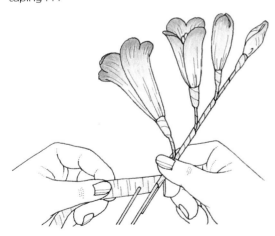

11 . . . through to extra-large. You may have to tape on an extra length of 20 gauge wire to extend the stem's overall length. If this is necessary, continue taping to the end of the stem.

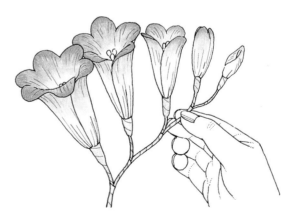

FINISHING OFF

12 Gently bend the stems of the flowers, to make the freesia look lifelike.

CARNATION

The colourful carnation is a very rewarding and easy flower to make. It is also extremely versatile and can be used almost anywhere, from corsages to table decorations.

Light-green and yellow handmade papers or
  fabrics
Light-green floral tape
20 gauge green covered wire
30 gauge wire
Cotton wool
Tools (scissors, ruler etc)

For one flower and one bud cut the following:

Part	Material	Quantity	Colour
Petal	handmade paper or fabric	8	yellow
Leaf	handmade paper or fabric	4	light green
Calyx	handmade paper or fabric	1	light green

The illustrated patterns are life-size. Trace them onto paper and use these templates to mark out the above parts of the flower. All techniques used here are fully described in General Materials and Techniques.

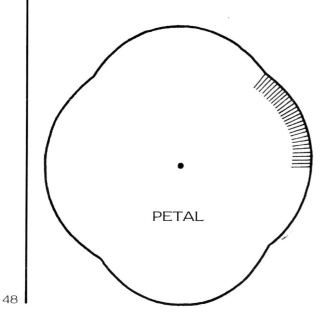

PETAL

LEAF

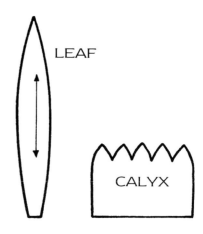

CALYX

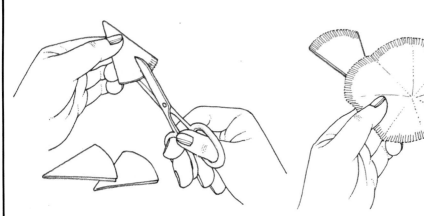
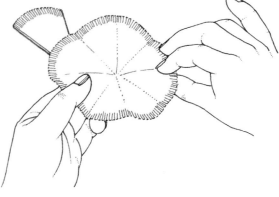

FLOWER

1 Fold each petal into eight and very finely fringe their open edges.

2 Open out the petals. Make sure that the fringing goes all the way around each one. If it does not, then refringe.

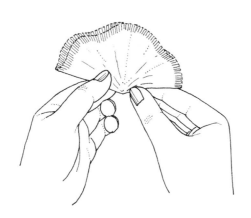

3 Fold one petal in half and make small, even gathers in the centre of its folded edge.

4 Starting about 1cm (½in) up from the petal's bottom point, firmly bind a short length of 30 gauge wire around the petal's base Tightly twist the two ends of wire, so fastening the gathers together. Tape around the binding, hiding it. Continue taping to the end of the wire. Repeat steps 3 and 4 with another petal.

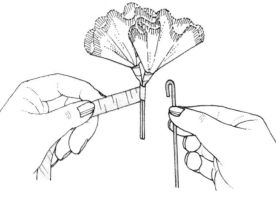

5 Cut an 8cm (3in) length of 20 gauge wire and bend a small hook into one end. Tape two petals together at their bases and hook the wire between them. Tape the petals and hooked wire together. Continue taping along the wire to a length of about 2cm (¾in).

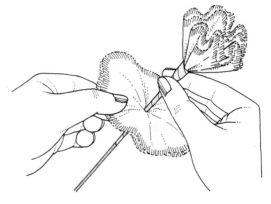

6 Pass the hooked wire through the centres of another two petals and position them underneath the previous ones.

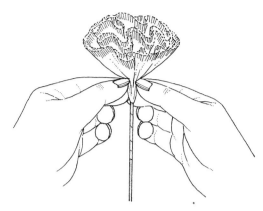

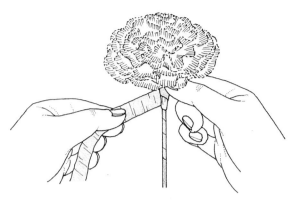

7 Pinch and gather together (from underneath) the centres of the petals, so making them dish-like in appearance. Tape around the gathers, fastening the petals onto the wire.

8 Repeat steps 6 and 7 with the remaining petals.

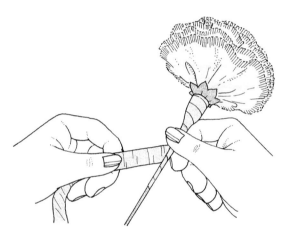

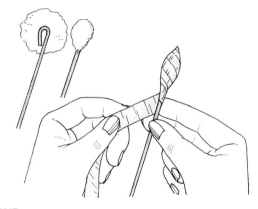

9 Tape the calyx around the flower's base. Continue taping to the end of the stem.

BUD

10 Make one little fingertip-sized, almond-shaped pompon consisting of a 10cm (4in) length of 20 gauge wire and a little cotton wool. Keeping its almond shape, wrap tape around the pompon, so fastening it onto the stem. Continue taping to the end of the stem.

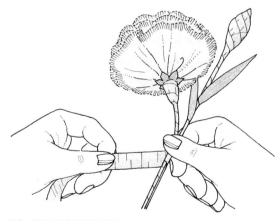

TO JOIN TOGETHER

11 About 3cm (1¼in) below the bud's base tape a leaf, at its base, around the stem. About 1cm (½in) further down tape another leaf, at its base, around the stem. Continue taping and add on the flower, so that it is about the same height as the bud. Continue taping . . .

12 . . . and, at the point where the flower joins onto the bud's stem, add on the remaining leaves, at their bases, around the stem. Continue taping to the end of the stem. Arrange to look lifelike.

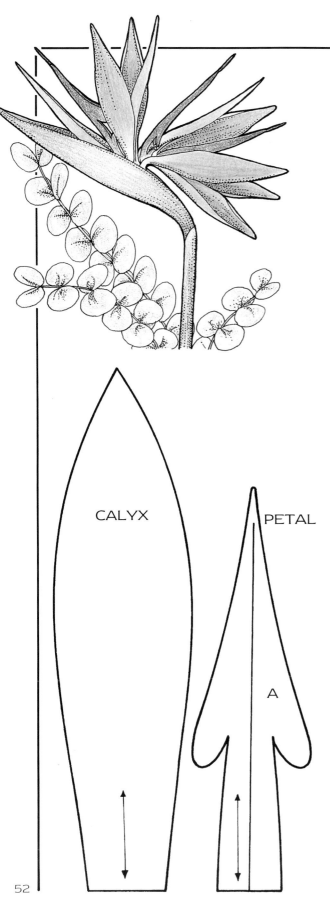

BIRD OF PARADISE
AND EUCALYPTUS

The exotic beauty of this bird of paradise and eucalyptus arrangement will bring the feeling of everlasting summer to your home.

Green, orange, purple and yellow crepe papers
Moss-green handmade paper or fabric
Green and moss-green floral tapes
18 gauge wire
28 gauge white covered wire
Purple and yellow felt-tip pens
A few tissues
PVA glue
Tools (scissors, ruler etc)

For one bird of paradise flower cut the following:

Part	Material	Quantity	Colour
Petal A	crepe paper	3	purple
Petal B	crepe paper	3	yellow
Petal C	crepe paper	7	orange
Calyx	crepe paper	2	green

The illustrated patterns for the bird of paradise's petals B and C can be found on page 54.

For one spray of eucalyptus cut the following:

Part	Material	Quantity	Colour
Leaf L	handmade paper or fabric	16	moss green
Leaf S	handmade paper or fabric	2	moss green

The illustrated patterns (page 54) are life-size. Trace them onto paper and use these templates to mark out the above parts of the flower. All techniques used here are fully described in General Materials and Techniques.

CALYX

PETAL

A

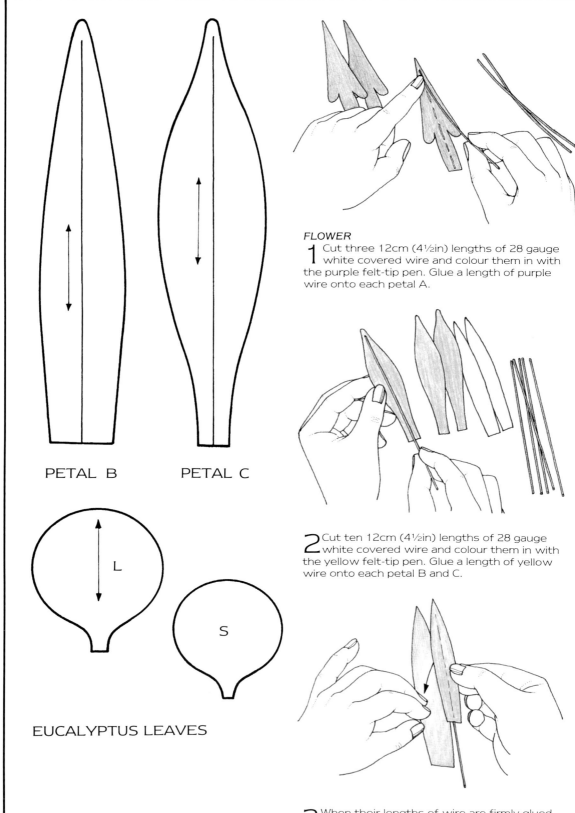

PETAL B   PETAL C

EUCALYPTUS LEAVES

FLOWER

1 Cut three 12cm (4½in) lengths of 28 gauge white covered wire and colour them in with the purple felt-tip pen. Glue a length of purple wire onto each petal A.

2 Cut ten 12cm (4½in) lengths of 28 gauge white covered wire and colour them in with the yellow felt-tip pen. Glue a length of yellow wire onto each petal B and C.

3 When their lengths of wire are firmly glued into place, glue one petal C (wired side facing downwards) centrally onto a calyx.

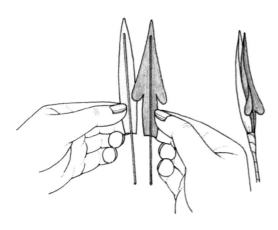

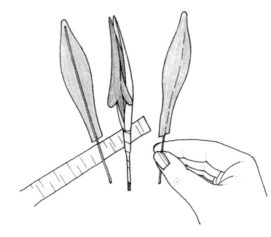

4 With their wired sides facing upwards, place one petal A on top of one petal B. Fasten the petals together at their bottom edges with green tape.

5 With their wired side facing inwards, place two petals C either side of the joined petals AB.

6 Tape AB and the two petals C together at their bottom edges, making one petal group. With the remaining petals A, B and C repeat steps 4 to 6.

7 Cut a 30cm (12in) length of 18 gauge wire and bend a small hook into one end. Tape the three petal groups together, each one slightly below the other. Hook the wire just above the base of the last petal group. Continue taping . . .

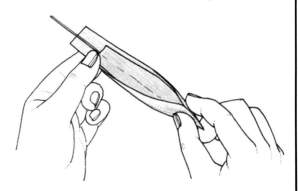

8 . . . and fasten the petal groups onto the hooked wire. Continue taping a little way along the wire.

9 With petal C on the inside, glue together just the sides of the calyx's tip.

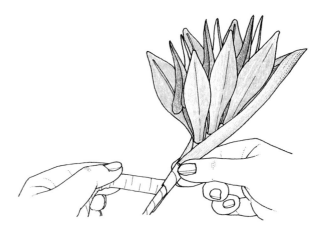

10 From behind, place the glued calyx around the base of the petal groups, so that the petal groups sit inside it.

11 Tape the calyx, at its base, around the stem.

12 From in front, place the remaining calyx around the stem, so that its tip just touches the other calyx's base.

13 Tape the calyx onto the stem.

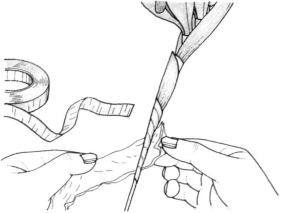

14 Tear up the tissues (along their length) into strips about 3cm (1¼in) wide. Thicken the bird of paradise's stem by wrapping it with the strips of tissue. Starting at the second calyx's base, neatly cover the tissue with tape. Continue taping to end of stem.

FINISHING OFF

15 At the joint of the two calyxes carefully curve the stem and open out the petals, to give the characteristic fan shape.

EUCALYPTUS

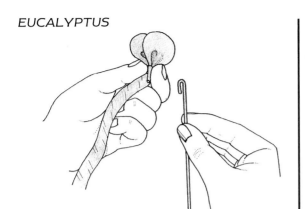

1 Cut a fairly long length of 18 gauge wire and bend a small hook into one end. Make small gathers in leaves S and fasten them together with moss-green tape. Hook the wire between leaves S. Tape the wire and leaves S together. Continue taping . . .

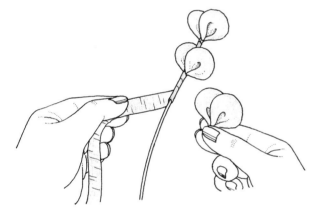

2 . . . and add on, one on either side of the wire and about 3cm (1 ¼in) apart, gathered pairs of leaves L. Continue taping and adding on gathered pairs of leaves until the end of the stem.

3 Carefully ease the leaves back from the stem and curve the stem.

IRIS (overleaf)

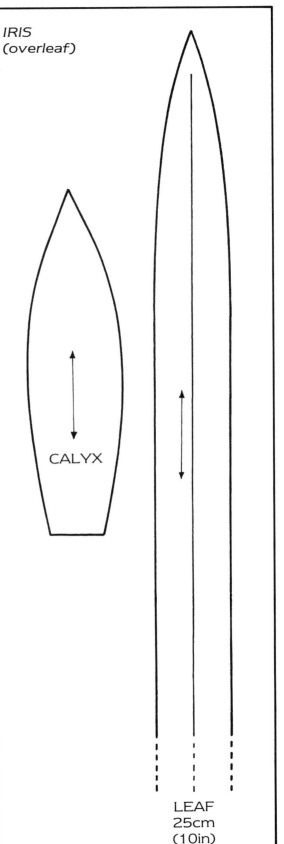

CALYX

LEAF
25cm
(10in)

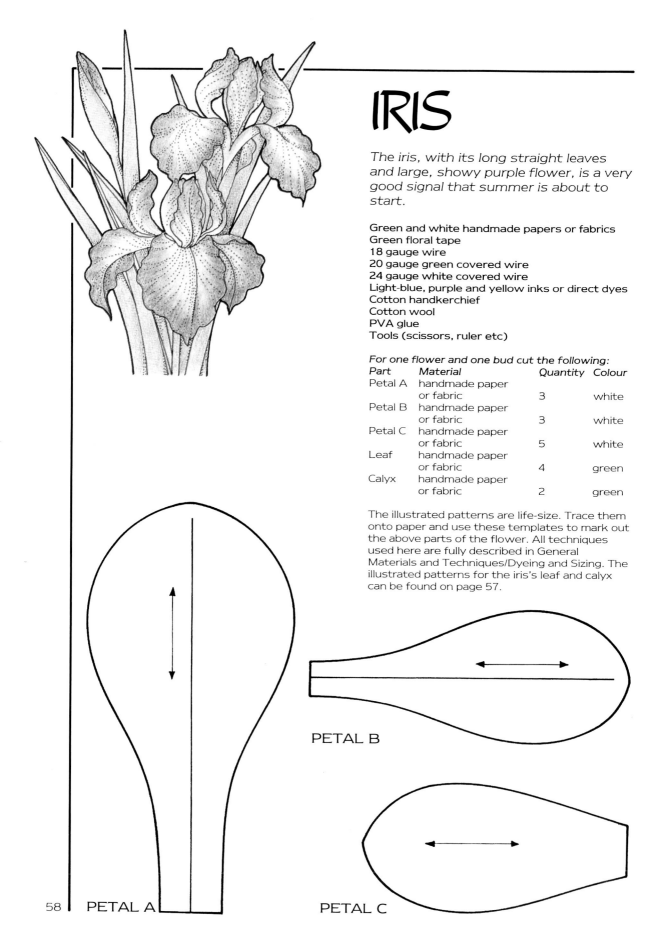

IRIS

The iris, with its long straight leaves and large, showy purple flower, is a very good signal that summer is about to start.

Green and white handmade papers or fabrics
Green floral tape
18 gauge wire
20 gauge green covered wire
24 gauge white covered wire
Light-blue, purple and yellow inks or direct dyes
Cotton handkerchief
Cotton wool
PVA glue
Tools (scissors, ruler etc)

For one flower and one bud cut the following:

Part	Material	Quantity	Colour
Petal A	handmade paper or fabric	3	white
Petal B	handmade paper or fabric	3	white
Petal C	handmade paper or fabric	5	white
Leaf	handmade paper or fabric	4	green
Calyx	handmade paper or fabric	2	green

The illustrated patterns are life-size. Trace them onto paper and use these templates to mark out the above parts of the flower. All techniques used here are fully described in General Materials and Techniques/Dyeing and Sizing. The illustrated patterns for the iris's leaf and calyx can be found on page 57.

PETAL B

PETAL C

PETAL A

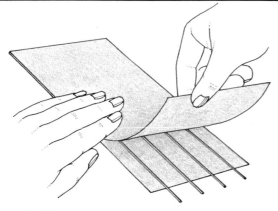
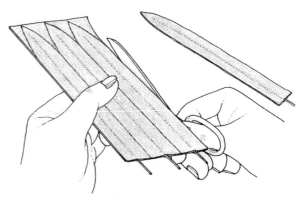

LEAVES

1 Cut four 25cm (10in) lengths of 20 gauge wire. Leaving a space of about 2cm (¾in) between each length of wire, glue them onto the green material. Glue another piece of green material on top of the lengths of wire.

2 When the lengths of wire are firmly glued into place, cut out the leaves.

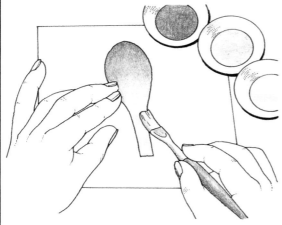
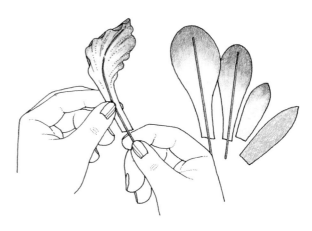

FLOWER

3 Using the technique for gradation dyeing, dye each petal. The ideal colouring, from top to bottom, should be purple gradually passing through to light blue, through to a small area of white and finally through to yellow.

4 Cut six 11cm (4½in) lengths of 24 gauge wire and, when the dye is dry, glue them onto petals A and B. Crinkle each calyx and the petals A, B and C.

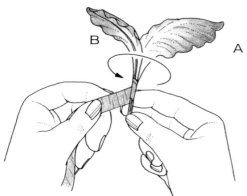
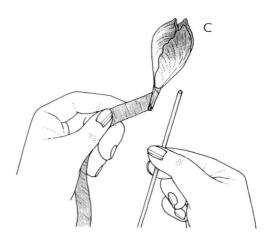

5 With their wired side facing outwards, place and tape together into a group, one petal A and one petal B. Repeat this step with the remaining petals A and B, so making two more groups.

IRIS CENTRE

6 With their cupped side facing inwards, tape together three petals C, so that they form a closed, cup-like shape. Tape the cupped petals C onto one end of a fairly long length of 18 gauge wire.

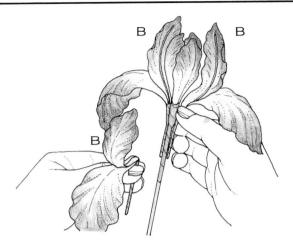

7 Being careful to have petals B facing inwards, tape the petal groups made in step 5 around the iris's centre.

8 With its cupped side facing inwards, place one calyx between two of the petals. Tape the calyx, at its base, around the stem. Continue taping to the end of the stem.

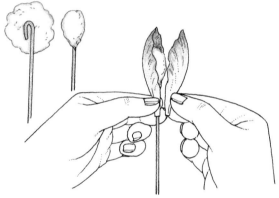

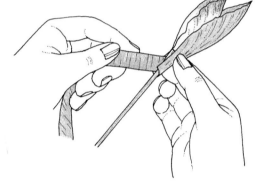

BUD

9 Make one thumbtip-sized pompon consisting of a 30cm (12in) length of 20 gauge wire and a little cotton wool. With their cupped side facing inwards, tape the remaining petals C around the pompon, so making a closed bud. Continue taping . . .

10 . . . and, with its cupped side facing inwards, add on the remaining calyx around the bud's base. Continue taping to the end of the stem.

11 Making sure that they are not any taller than the bud, tape two of the leaves, at their bases, around the stem. Continue taping to the end of the stem.

12 Making sure that they are not any taller than the flower, tape the remaining leaves, at their bases, around the stem. Continue taping to the end of the stem.

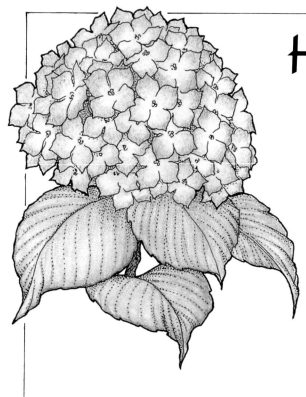

HYDRANGEA

The large cluster of variegated flowers and toothed oval leaves that comprise the hydrangea are very easy and simple to make.

Green and white handmade papers or fabrics
Light-green and olive-green floral tapes
18 and 24 gauge green covered wires
80 yellow stamens
Blue, pink, purple and yellow inks or direct dyes
PVA glue
Tools (scissors, ruler etc)
Before you start to cut the petals out, dye the white material in hydrangea colours.

For one hydrangea cut the following:

Part	Material	Quantity	Colour
Petal L	handmade paper or fabric	32	hydrangea
Petal M	handmade paper or fabric	32	hydrangea
Petal S	handmade paper or fabric	16	hydrangea
Leaves L/M/S	handmade paper or fabric	2 of each	green

The illustrated patterns are life-size. Trace them onto paper and use these templates to mark out the above parts of the flower. All techniques used here are fully described in General Materials and Techniques/Dyeing and Sizing.

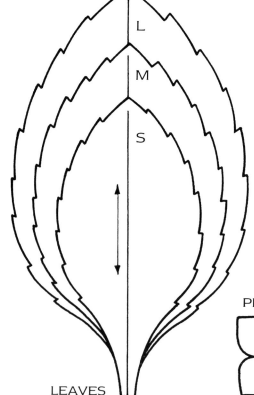

L

M

S

LEAVES

PETALS

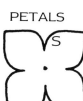

S

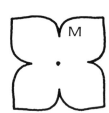

M

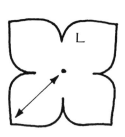

L

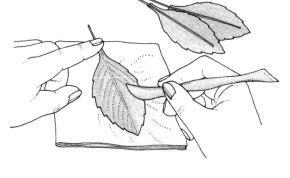

LEAVES

1 From the 24 gauge wire cut six lengths just a little shorter than the lengths of the leaves. Glue the lengths of wire onto their respective leaves.

2 Emboss each leaf.

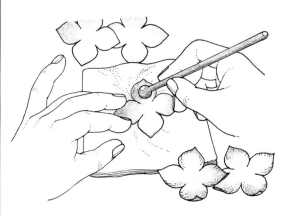
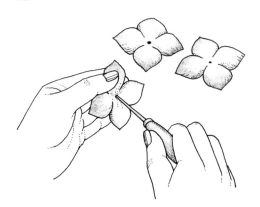

4 With a sharp pointed tool make a tiny hole in the centre of each petal.

FLOWER

3 Cup each petal.

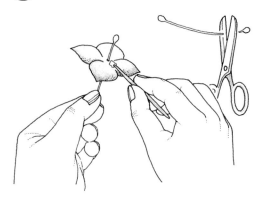
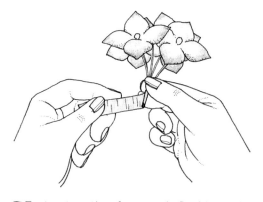

5 Cut off and discard the head at one end of a stamen. With one petal's cupped side facing downwards, place a little glue around its centre hole. Pass the stamen's stem through the centre hole, so that its remaining head sits in the petal's centre. Repeat this step with the remaining petals, taking care that they do not get mixed up.

6 Fasten together four petals S with the light-green tape, making one small petal group. Repeat this step with the remaining petals S, making three more groups.

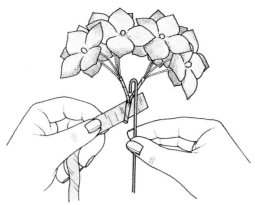

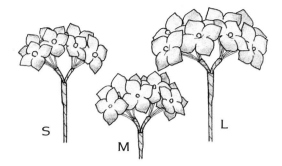

7 Cut a 12cm (4½in) length of 24 gauge wire and bend a small hook into one end. Tape together two small petal groups and hook the wire between them. Tape the petal groups and hooked wire together. Continue taping to the end of the wire, so making one small flower head. Repeat this step with the remaining small petal groups.

8 Being very careful not to get them mixed up, repeat steps 6 and 7 with petals M and L. The end result of this patient work should be two small flower heads, four medium flower heads and four large flower heads.

TO JOIN TOGETHER

9 Cut a fairly long length of 18 gauge wire and bend a small hook into one end. About 3cm (1¼in) below their flowers, tape the small flower heads together and hook the wire between them. Tape together the flower heads and hooked wire. Continue taping for a further 4cm (1½in) along the wire.

10 About 3cm (1¼in) down from where the small flower heads are taped together, fasten the medium flower heads (about 6cm (2¼in) below their flowers) onto the main stem with olive-green tape. Bend their stems over a little, positioning the medium flower heads next to the small flower heads.

11 At the point where the medium flower heads join the main stem, repeat step 10 with the large flowers, so making the hydrangea's ball-shaped head. Continue taping along the stem . . .

12 . . . and add on the leaves, each about 4cm (1½in) apart, making sure that they range from S through to L. Continue taping to the end of the stem. Curl the leaves outwards.

FOXGLOVE

The foxglove, with its tall straight stem and thimble-shaped flowers, is an ideal plant for the kitchen window ledge.

Green handmade paper or fabric
Pink crepe paper
Green floral tape
20 and 24 gauge green covered wires
Brown felt-tip pen
PVA glue
Tools (scissors, ruler etc)

For one foxglove cut the following (To make the arrangement in the photograph, increase the number of petals and calyxes):

Part	Material	Quantity	Colour
Petals L/M	crepe paper	2 of each	pink
Petal S	crepe paper	4	pink
Leaves L/S	handmade paper or fabric	2 of each	green
Calyx	handmade paper or fabric	8	green

The illustrated patterns are life-size. Trace them onto paper and use these templates to mark out the above parts of the flower. All techniques used here are fully described in General Materials and Techniques.

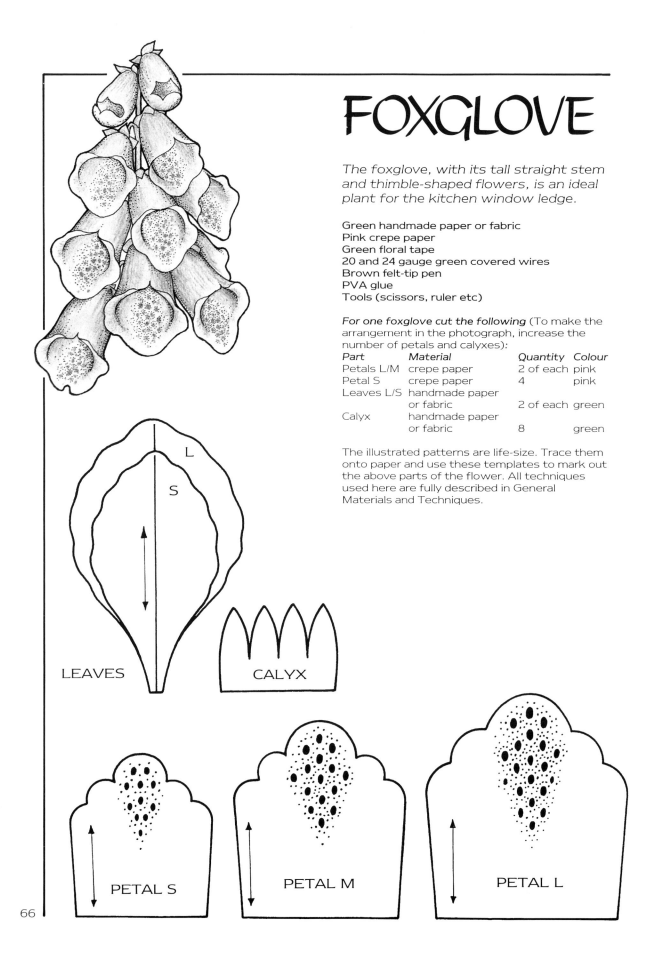

LEAVES

CALYX

PETAL S

PETAL M

PETAL L

66

FOXGLOVE

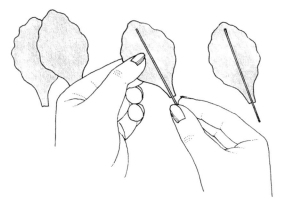

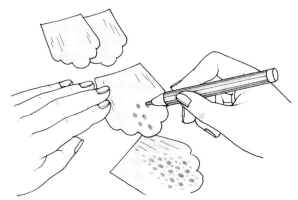

LEAVES

1 Glue a 10cm (4in) length of 24 gauge wire onto each leaf.

FLOWER

2 As illustrated, speckle each petal with the brown felt-tip pen.

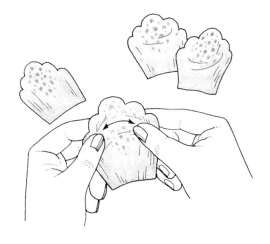

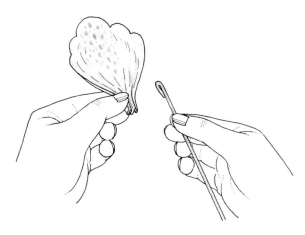

3 With their speckled side facing upwards, stretch cup petals M and L.

4 With its cupped side facing upwards, make small, even gathers along one petal M's bottom edge, making it fan-like. Cut a 6cm (2¼in) length from the 24 gauge wire and bend a small hook into one end. Place the hooked wire onto the petal.

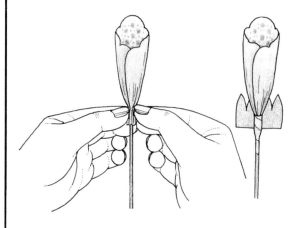

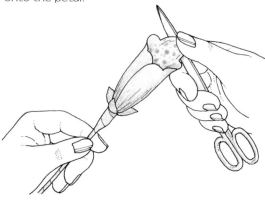

5 Wrap the petal around the hook, so that its sides overlap slightly. Tape around the petal's base, so fastening it onto the hooked wire. Tape one calyx around the petal's base. Continue taping to the end of the stem.

6 Curl the petal's tips outwards. Repeat steps 4 to 6 with the remaining petals M and L.

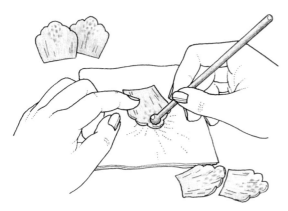

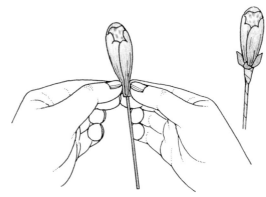

7 With their speckled side facing upwards, cup petals S.

8 With cupped petals S repeat steps 4 and 5.

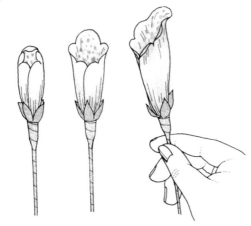

9 The end result of this patient work should be four small flowers, two medium flowers and two large flowers.

TO JOIN TOGETHER

10 Tape two small flowers onto one end of a fairly long length of 20 gauge wire. Continue taping . . .

11 . . . and add on the remaining flowers (so that their overlapping side is against the stem) each about 1cm (½in) apart, making sure that they range from small through to large. Continue taping and add on the leaves, making sure that they range from S through to L. Continue taping to the end of the stem.

FINISHING OFF

12 Bend the leaves outwards and bend the flowers gently down, to show their brown speckles.

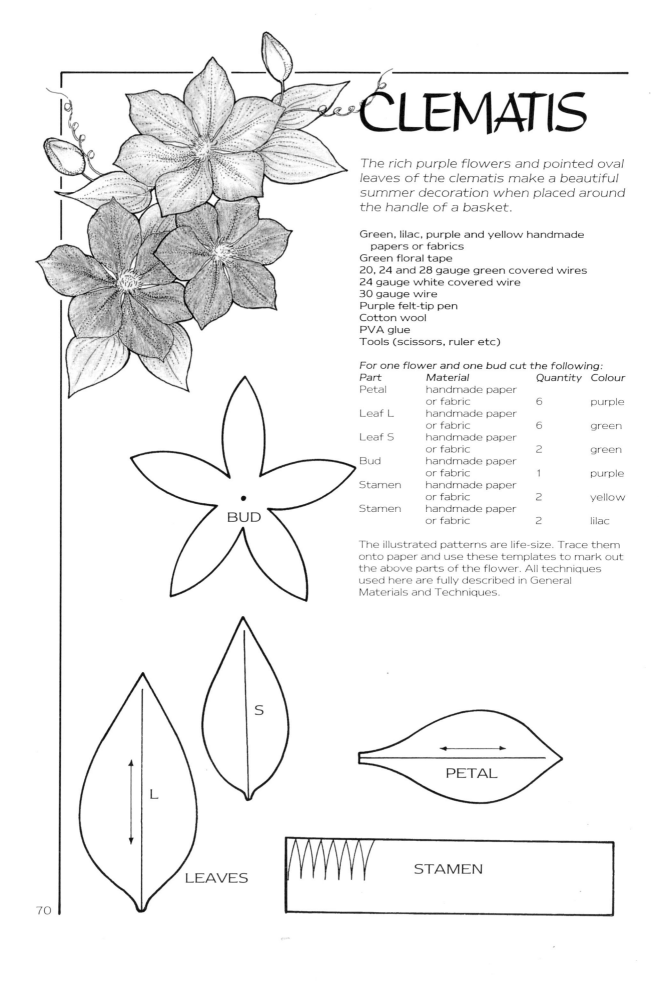

CLEMATIS

The rich purple flowers and pointed oval leaves of the clematis make a beautiful summer decoration when placed around the handle of a basket.

Green, lilac, purple and yellow handmade
  papers or fabrics
Green floral tape
20, 24 and 28 gauge green covered wires
24 gauge white covered wire
30 gauge wire
Purple felt-tip pen
Cotton wool
PVA glue
Tools (scissors, ruler etc)

For one flower and one bud cut the following:

Part	Material	Quantity	Colour
Petal	handmade paper or fabric	6	purple
Leaf L	handmade paper or fabric	6	green
Leaf S	handmade paper or fabric	2	green
Bud	handmade paper or fabric	1	purple
Stamen	handmade paper or fabric	2	yellow
Stamen	handmade paper or fabric	2	lilac

The illustrated patterns are life-size. Trace them onto paper and use these templates to mark out the above parts of the flower. All techniques used here are fully described in General Materials and Techniques.

BUD

LEAVES

S

L

PETAL

STAMEN

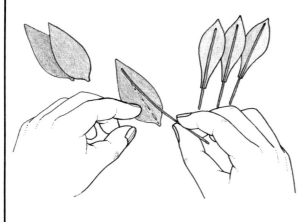
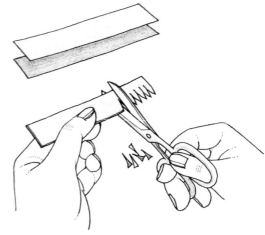

PETALS AND LEAVES

1 Cut six 8cm (3in) lengths of 24 gauge white covered wire and colour them in with the purple felt-tip pen. Glue a length of purple wire onto each petal. Glue an 8cm (3in) length of 24 gauge green covered wire onto each leaf.

STAMENS

2 Make two sets, each one consisting of a yellow and lilac stamen glued together. Serrate the stamens as illustrated.

BUD

3 Make one good almond-sized pompon consisting of an 8cm (3in) length of 24 gauge green covered wire and a little cotton wool.

4 Pass the pompon's wire through the bud's centre.

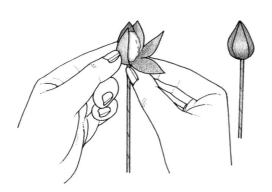
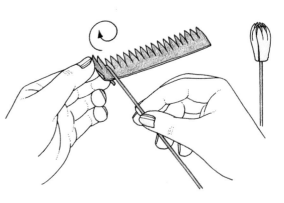

5 With the aid of a little glue, wrap the pompon inside the bud's petals.

FLOWER

6 Cut a 10cm (4in) length of 20 gauge wire and bend a small hook into one end. Spread a little glue along the bottom edge of one stamen and hook the wire into one end. Roll the stamen tightly around the wire, with lilac on the inside and yellow on the outside. Fasten the end with a little glue. Gently tap the stamen's top, making it curl inwards.

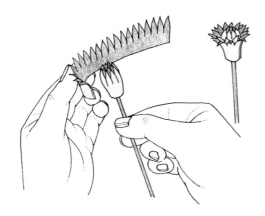

7 Spread a little glue along the bottom edge of the remaining stamen and, making sure that you have lilac on the inside and yellow on the outside, roll it around the one that you have just made. Fasten the end with a little glue. Gently curl this stamen's top outwards.

8 With their wired side facing outwards, place, in turn, the six petals around the stamen and twist their protruding wires tightly around the stem.

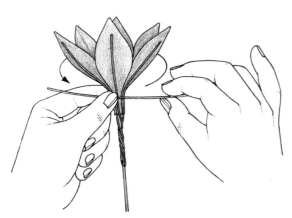

9 Starting about 1cm (½in) up from the bottom of the petals, firmly bind a short length of 30 gauge wire around their base, fastening them together and, at the same time, onto the stem.

10 Tape around the binding, hiding it. Continue taping to the end of the stem.

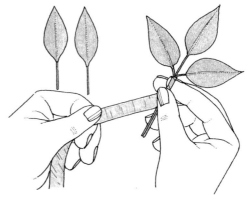

11 Very gently, open out the petals one by one, making them into the shape of a clematis flower.

LEAVES

12 Making sure that their wired side is facing downwards, tape together leaves L into two units of three.

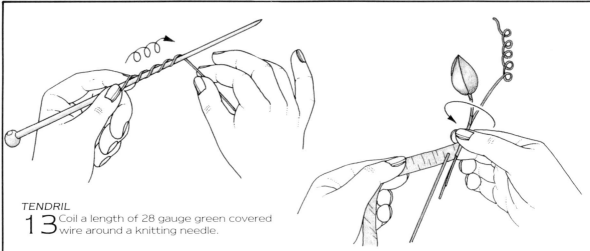

TENDRIL

13 Coil a length of 28 gauge green covered wire around a knitting needle.

TO JOIN TOGETHER

14 Tape the tendril and bud onto a 20cm (8in) length of 20 gauge wire, one slightly above the other. Continue taping . . .

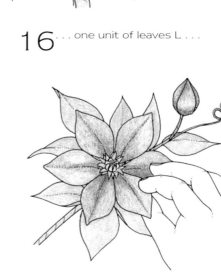

15 . . . and add on leaves S, each about 2cm (¾in) apart . . .

16 . . . one unit of leaves L . . .

17 . . . the flower and the remaining unit of leaves L. Continue taping to the end of the stem.

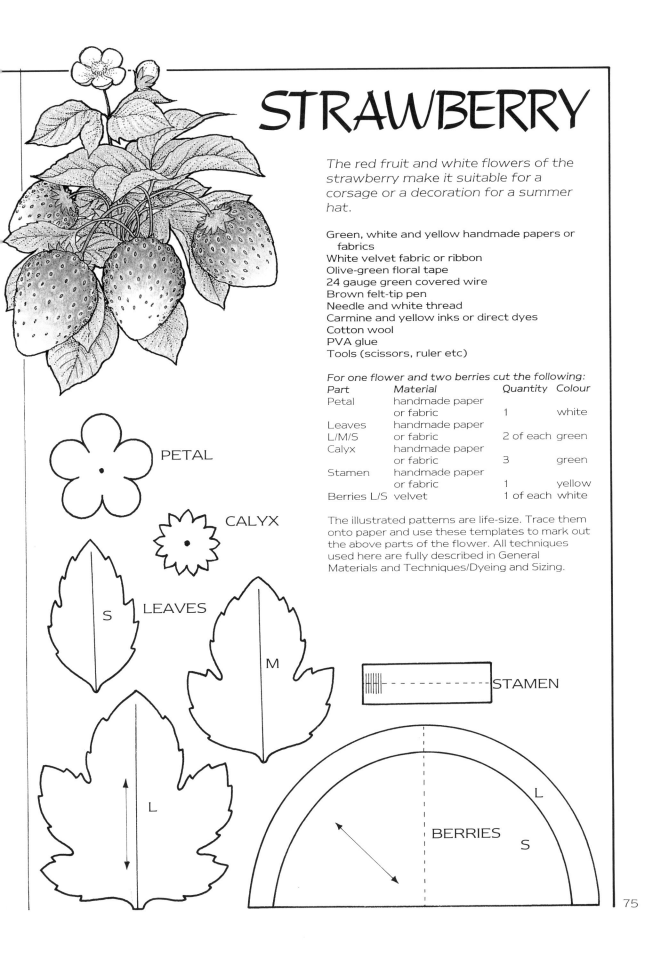

STRAWBERRY

The red fruit and white flowers of the strawberry make it suitable for a corsage or a decoration for a summer hat.

Green, white and yellow handmade papers or
　fabrics
White velvet fabric or ribbon
Olive-green floral tape
24 gauge green covered wire
Brown felt-tip pen
Needle and white thread
Carmine and yellow inks or direct dyes
Cotton wool
PVA glue
Tools (scissors, ruler etc)

For one flower and two berries cut the following:

Part	Material	Quantity	Colour
Petal	handmade paper or fabric	1	white
Leaves L/M/S	handmade paper or fabric	2 of each	green
Calyx	handmade paper or fabric	3	green
Stamen	handmade paper or fabric	1	yellow
Berries L/S	velvet	1 of each	white

The illustrated patterns are life-size. Trace them onto paper and use these templates to mark out the above parts of the flower. All techniques used here are fully described in General Materials and Techniques/Dyeing and Sizing.

PETAL

CALYX

LEAVES

S

M

L

STAMEN

BERRIES

L

S

75

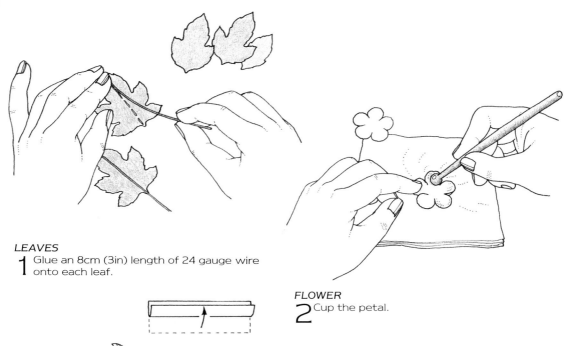

LEAVES

1 Glue an 8cm (3in) length of 24 gauge wire onto each leaf.

FLOWER

2 Cup the petal.

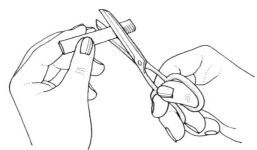

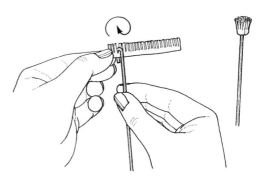

3 Fold the stamen in half lengthways and cut a tiny fringe along its folded edge. Be careful not to cut right through to the opened edges.

4 Cut a 12cm (4½in) length from the 24 gauge wire and bend a small hook into one end. Spread a little glue along the stamen's opened edges and hook the wire into one end. Roll the stamen tightly around the wire. Fasten the end with a little glue.

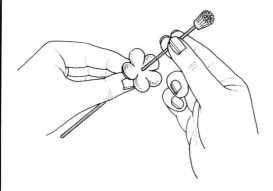

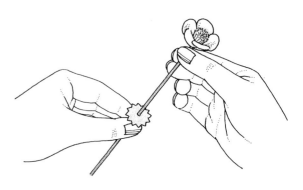

5 Place a little glue onto the stamen's bottom. With the petal's cupped side facing upwards pass the stamen's wire through the petal's centre, so gluing the stamen onto the petal.

6 Place a little glue around one calyx's centre. Pass the petal's wire through the calyx's centre, gluing the petal onto the calyx.

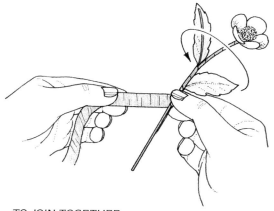

TO JOIN TOGETHER

7 Starting adjacent to the calyx's base tape along the stem, turning the stem 'into' the tape, as illustrated. About 2cm (¾in) below the flower's base tape one leaf S onto the stem. Continue taping and, each about 1cm (½in) apart, add on the remaining leaf S . . .

8 . . . leaves M and one leaf L. Continue taping to the end of the stem.

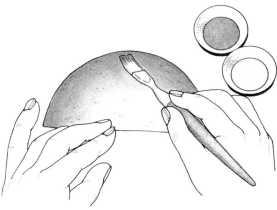

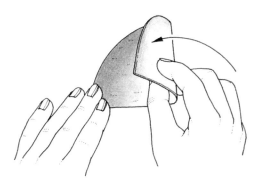

10 When it is dry, fold berry L in half from side to side with the velvet side on top.

BERRIES

9 Using the gradation dyeing technique, dye berry L on its velvet side. The ideal colouring, from the outer edge towards the bottom centre, should be carmine gradually passing through to yellow and then through to white.

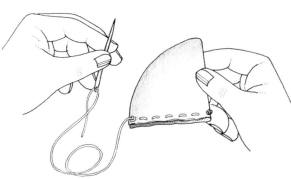

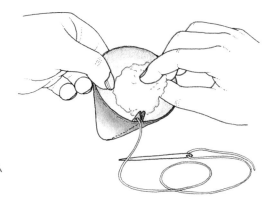

11 Using the needle and white cotton, sew berry L's bottom edges together, starting from the folded side. When you come to the end, do not cut the cotton, but make a small knot.

12 Turn berry L inside out, to make a cone. Approximately half fill the cone with cotton wool.

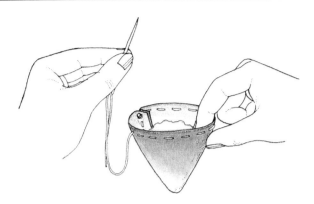

13 With as tiny stitches as possible, sew around the cone's top edge, leaving a long end.

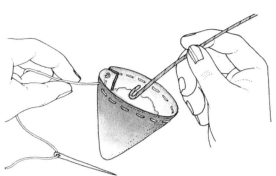

14 Cut a 10cm (4in) length of 24 gauge wire and bend a small hook into one end. Insert the hook deep into the cotton wool.

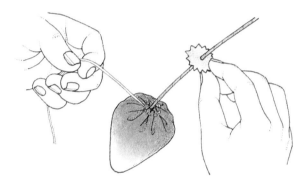

15 Pull the cotton, closing up the cone. Fasten the cotton off. Place a little glue around the centre of one calyx. Pass the berry's wire through the calyx's centre and glue it onto the berry.

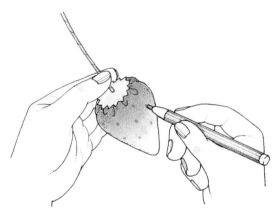

16 With the brown felt-tip pen draw on the strawberry's seeds. Repeat steps 9 to 16 with berry S.

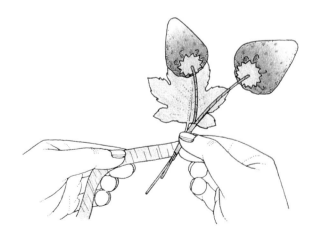

TO JOIN TOGETHER

17 Tape together the remaining leaf L and strawberries.

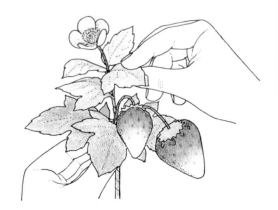

18 Tape the strawberries underneath the flower's leaves. Continue taping to the end of the stem and arrange to look lifelike.

SALVIA

The brilliant red flowers and grey-green leaves of the salvia look splendid on the kitchen window ledge, arranged in a clay flowerpot.

Green and red handmade papers or fabrics
Brown and light-green floral tapes
20 and 24 gauge green covered wires
7 red-headed stamens (or white ones, dyed)
14 yellow stamens
Cotton wool
PVA glue
Tools (scissors, ruler etc)

For one stem of salvia cut the following (to make the arrangement in the photograph, increase the number of petals and leaves):

Part	Material	Quantity	Colour
Petal L	handmade paper or fabric	3	red
Petal M	handmade paper or fabric	7	red
Petal S	handmade paper or fabric	3	red
Leaves L/M/S	handmade paper or fabric	2 of each	green

The illustrated patterns are life-size. Trace them onto paper and use these templates to mark out the above parts of the flower. All techniques used here are fully described in General Materials and Techniques/Dyeing and Sizing.

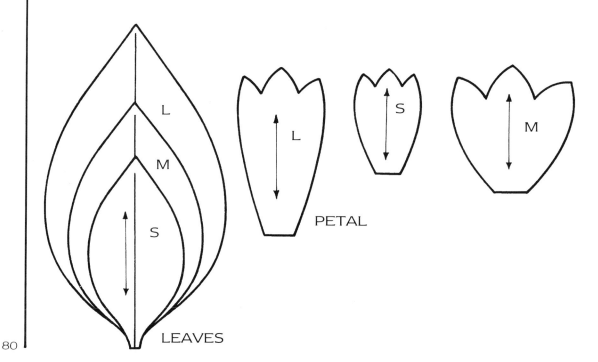

LEAVES

PETAL

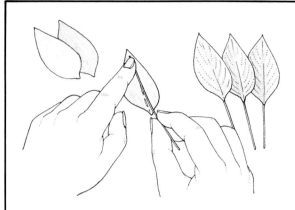

LEAVES

1 Glue a 10cm (4in) length of 24 gauge wire onto each leaf. Emboss each leaf.

PETALS

3 Cup each petal.

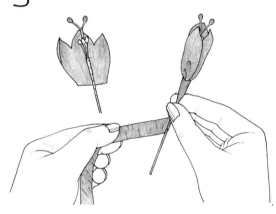

MEDIUM FLOWERS

5 With its cupped side facing upwards, place a flower centre onto a petal M, so that the Y stamen slightly protrudes. Wrap the petal around the flower centre, so that its sides overlap slightly. Fasten the petal onto the stem with a length of brown tape. Repeat this step with three more petals M.

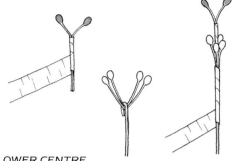

FLOWER CENTRE

2 Bend the seven red-headed stamens in half and make each one resemble the letter Y. Bind with a small length of light-green tape.

Make seven flower centres, each one consisting of an 8cm (3in) length of 24 gauge wire and two yellow stamens. Making sure that the Y stamen protrudes 1cm (½in) above the yellow stamens, tape together, at their bases, one flower centre and one Y stamen. Continue taping to the end of the wire. Repeat this step with the remaining Y stamens and flower centres.

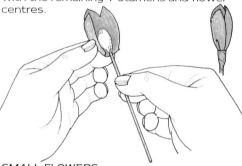

SMALL FLOWERS

4 Make one little fingertip-sized pompon consisting of an 8cm (3in) length of 24 gauge wire and a little cotton wool. With its cupped side facing inwards wrap a petal S around the pompon, so that its sides overlap slightly. Fasten the petal onto the stem with a length of brown tape. Repeat this step with the remaining petals S.

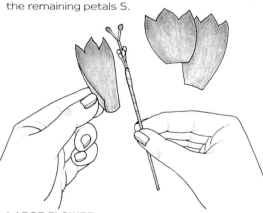

LARGE FLOWER

6 With its cupped side facing upwards, place a flower centre onto a petal L, so that the Y stamen slightly protrudes. Wrap the petal around the flower centre, so that its sides overlap slightly. Glue the overlapping sides together.

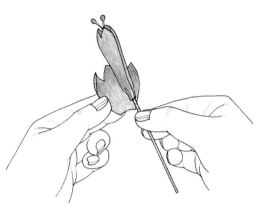

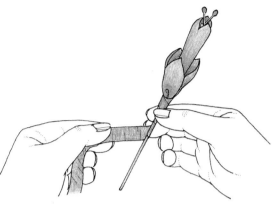

7 With its cupped side facing inwards, wrap a petal M around the large flower's base.

8 Tape around petal M's base, fastening it and the large flower onto the stem. Repeat steps 6 to 8 with the remaining petals M and L. The end result of this patient work should be three small flowers, four medium flowers and three large flowers.

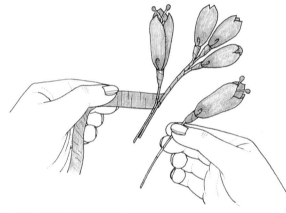

TO JOIN TOGETHER

9 With each one slightly below the other, fasten together the small flowers, medium flowers . . .

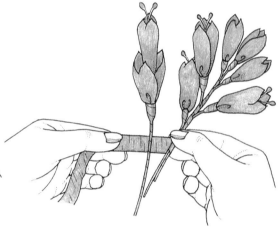

10 . . . and large flowers with brown tape. Continue taping along the stem to a length of about 3cm (1 ¼in).

11 About 2cm (¾in) below the final large flower fasten the leaves onto the stem with light-green tape. Make sure that the leaves range from S through to L. Continue taping to the end of the stem.

FINISHING OFF

12 Gently bend the flowers down, so that they stand out from the stem.

PETUNIA

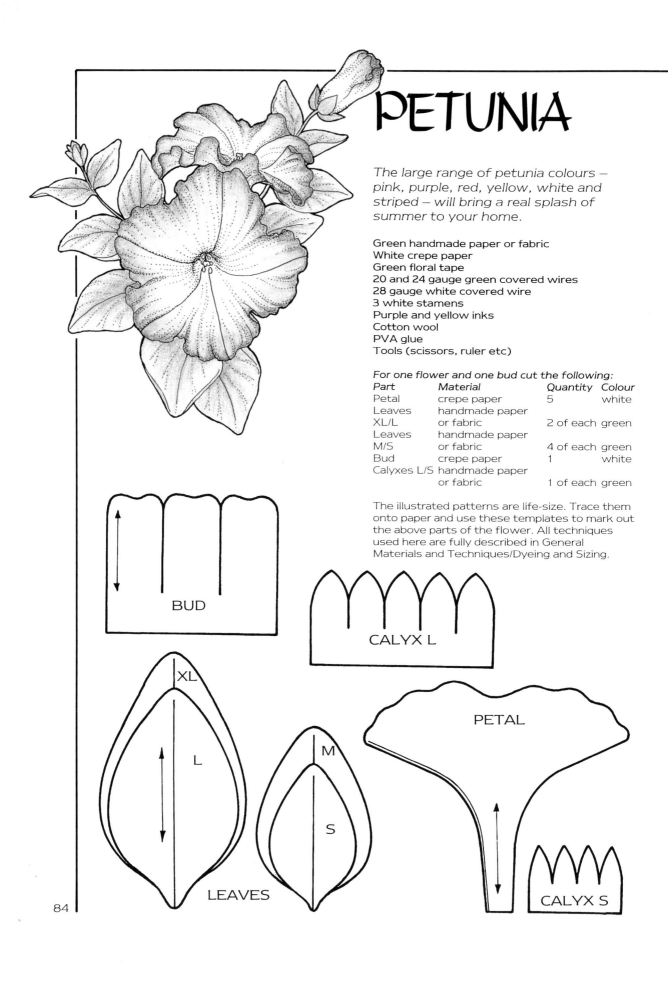

*The large range of petunia colours —
pink, purple, red, yellow, white and
striped — will bring a real splash of
summer to your home.*

Green handmade paper or fabric
White crepe paper
Green floral tape
20 and 24 gauge green covered wires
28 gauge white covered wire
3 white stamens
Purple and yellow inks
Cotton wool
PVA glue
Tools (scissors, ruler etc)

For one flower and one bud cut the following:

Part	Material	Quantity	Colour
Petal	crepe paper	5	white
Leaves XL/L	handmade paper or fabric	2 of each	green
Leaves M/S	handmade paper or fabric	4 of each	green
Bud	crepe paper	1	white
Calyxes L/S	handmade paper or fabric	1 of each	green

The illustrated patterns are life-size. Trace them
onto paper and use these templates to mark out
the above parts of the flower. All techniques
used here are fully described in General
Materials and Techniques/Dyeing and Sizing.

BUD

CALYX L

XL

L

M

S

PETAL

LEAVES

CALYX S

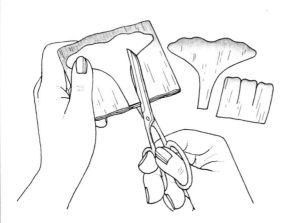

FLOWER

1 Using the dyeing technique for crepe paper, dye the top and bottom of the white crepe paper. The ideal colouring should be purple at the top and yellow at the bottom, with the centre being left white. Being careful to have the purple dyed area at the top, cut out the petals and bud.

2 Around the left-hand side of each petal glue on an 8cm (3in) length of 28 gauge white covered wire. Before progressing to the next step make sure that the lengths of wire are firmly glued into place.

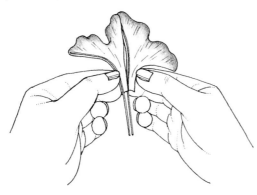

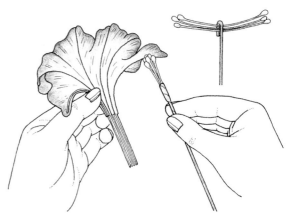

3 Place a little glue along the wired edge of each petal. Join the petals together, to make an *open* trumpet-like shape.

4 Make one flower centre consisting of a 10cm (4in) length of 24 gauge green covered wire, the three white stamens and a length of tape.

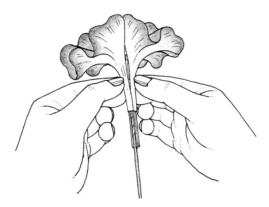

5 With the flower centre on the inside, glue the remaining petal edges together, so closing the trumpet.

6 Make small, even gathers along calyx L's bottom edge. Being careful not to let go of the gathers, wrap calyx L around the closed trumpet's base.

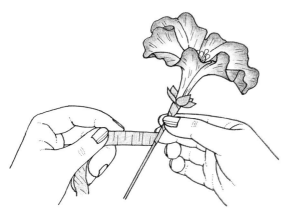

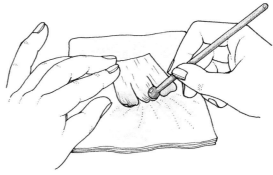

7 Tape around calyx L's base, to fasten it and the petals onto the stem. Continue taping to the end of the stem.

BUD
8 Cup the bud's tips.

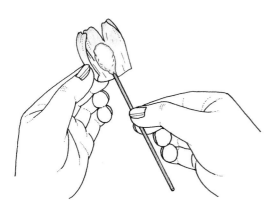

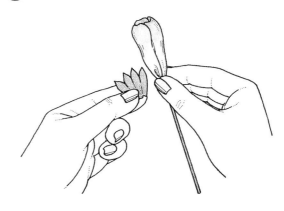

9 Make one little fingertip-sized pompon consisting of a 10cm (4in) length of 24 gauge wire and a little cotton wool. With its cupped tips facing inwards, wrap the bud around the pompon.

10 Wrap calyx S around the bud's base.

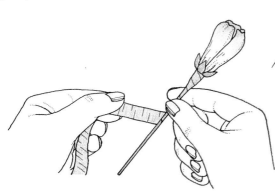

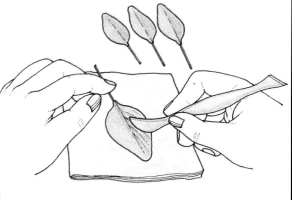

11 Tape around calyx S's base, to fasten it and the bud onto the stem.

LEAVES
12 Glue an 8cm (3in) length of 24 gauge wire onto each leaf. Emboss each leaf.

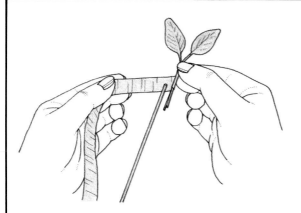

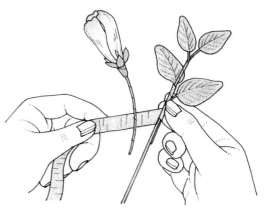

TO JOIN TOGETHER

13 Tape two leaves S onto one end of a 15cm (6in) length of 20 gauge wire. Continue taping . . .

14 . . . and add on two leaves M and the bud, each about 2cm (¾in) apart. Continue taping . . .

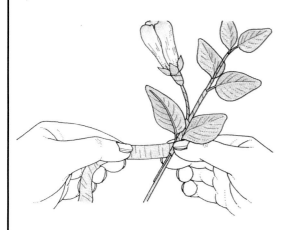

15 . . . and, at the point where the bud joins onto the main stem, add on leaves L. Continue taping to the end of the stem.

16 Repeat steps 13 and 14 with the remaining leaves S and M, but add on the flower in place of the bud.

17 Tape together the bud and flower stems. Continue taping . . .

18 . . . and, to hide the joint where the two stems meet, add on leaves XL. Continue taping to the end of the stem.

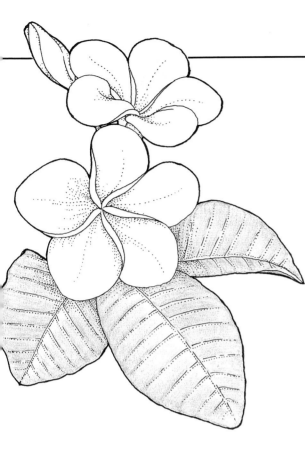

FRANGIPANI

The frangipani brings the feeling of everlasting tropical summers. An ideal flower to have on your window ledge or balcony, or in a corsage or bouquet.

White velvet fabric or ribbon
White floral tape
20 and 24 gauge white covered wires
30 gauge wire
Yellow ink or direct dye
PVA glue
Tools (scissors, ruler etc)

For one large flower, one small flower and two buds cut the following:

Part	Material	Quantity	Colour
Petal L	velvet	5	white
Petal S	velvet	5	white
Bud	velvet	2	white

The illustrated patterns are life-size. Trace them onto paper and use these templates to mark out the above parts of the flower. All techniques used here are fully described in General Materials and Techniques/Dyeing and Sizing/ Assembling a Bridal Bouquet and Corsage.

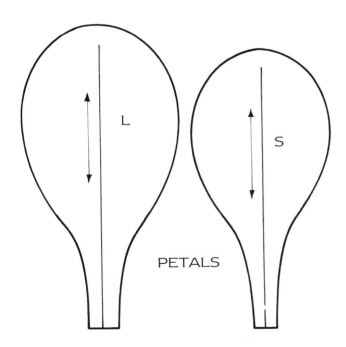

L

S

PETALS

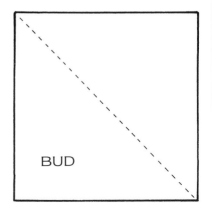

BUD

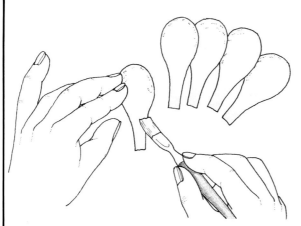
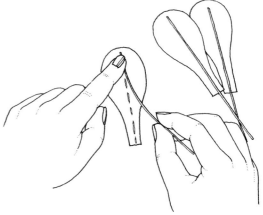

FLOWER

1 Using the gradation dyeing techniques, dye the petals on their velvet side. The ideal colouring, from top to bottom, should be white gradually passing through to yellow. Before progressing to the next step make sure that the petals are dry.

2 With their non-velvet side facing upwards, glue an 8cm (3in) length of 24 gauge wire onto each petal. Before progressing to the next step make sure that the lengths of wire are firmly glued into place.

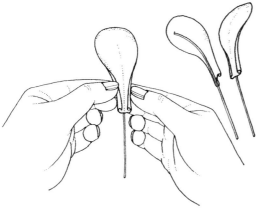
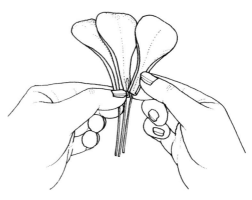

3 With their velvet side facing upwards, gently roll the side edges of each petal towards the centre, between your thumbs and forefingers.

4 Place a little glue on the bottom of petals L and, with their wired side facing outwards, join them together, so that they overlap . . .

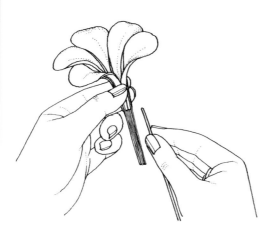
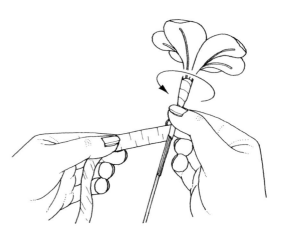

5 . . . to make a trumpet-like shape. Cut a 6cm (2¼in) length of 20 gauge wire and insert it inside the base of the petals.

6 Tape around the base of the petals, to fasten them onto the wire. Continue taping to the end of the stem.

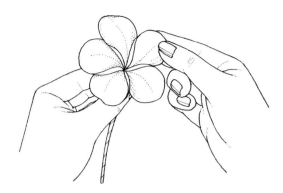

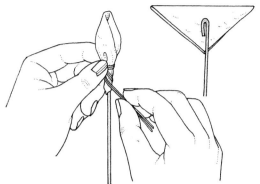

7 Very gently, open out the petals one by one, making them into the shape of a large frangipani flower. Repeat steps 4 to 7 with petals S, to make a small frangipani flower.

BUD

8 Being careful that each finished bud has the velvet side of the material facing outwards, make two buds, each one consisting of a 10cm (4in) length of 20 gauge wire, a bud and a small length of 30 gauge wire.

FRANGIPANI CORSAGE

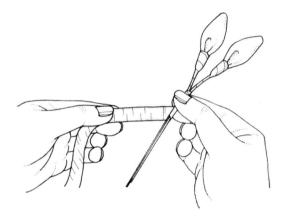

9 Tape the buds together. Continue taping to the end of the stem.

1 Make twelve all-white strawberry flowers (p75). Tape them together into four groups of three and then into two groups of six.

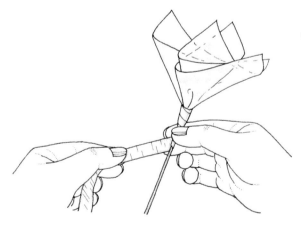

2 Make a tulle decoration out of a 12cm (4½in) square.

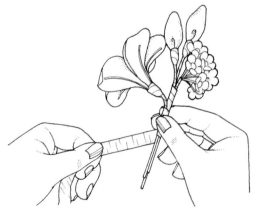

3 Tape together two frangipani buds, one group of strawberry flowers and one small frangipani flower. Continue taping . . .

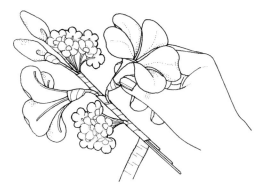

4 . . . and add on a large frangipani flower and the remaining group of strawberry flowers. Continue taping . . .

5 . . . and add on the tulle decoration and a ribbon decoration. Continue taping to the end of the corsage's wires, to make a small handle.

FRANGIPANI BOUQUET

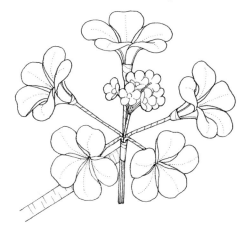

1 Make thirty-six all-white strawberry flowers (p75) and tape them together into six groups of six. Make five large frangipani flowers, giving each one in step 5 a 20cm (8in) length of 20 gauge wire. Also make two frangipani buds. At about 8cm (3in) down from their bases, tape together one strawberry flower group and the five frangipani flowers.

2 Tape and fill in with the remaining strawberry flower groups. Continue taping . . .

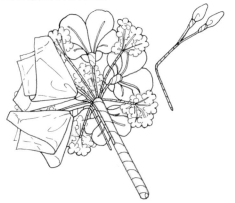

3 . . . and add on the buds and six to eight tulle decorations. Continue taping to the end of the bouquet's wires, to make a handle.

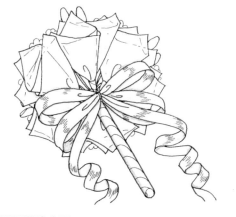

FINISHING OFF

4 Add a ribbon decoration and arrange the bouquet to suit personal taste.

LILY

The lily is a true aristocrat among flowers. Its dramatic yellow colouring makes it ideal for 'Ikebana'.

Green and yellow handmade papers or fabrics
Green and white floral tapes
20 and 24 gauge green covered wires
24 gauge white covered wire
3 brown stamens
3 white stamens
Brown and yellow felt-tip pens
Cotton wool
PVA glue
Tools (scissors, ruler etc)

For one flower and one bud cut the following:

Part	Material	Quantity	Colour
Petal	handmade paper or fabric	6	yellow
Leaf L	handmade paper or fabric	2	green
Leaf S	handmade paper or fabric	3	green
Bud	handmade paper or fabric	3	yellow

The illustrated patterns are life-size. Trace them onto paper and use these templates to mark out the above parts of the flower. All techniques used here are fully described in General Materials and Techniques.

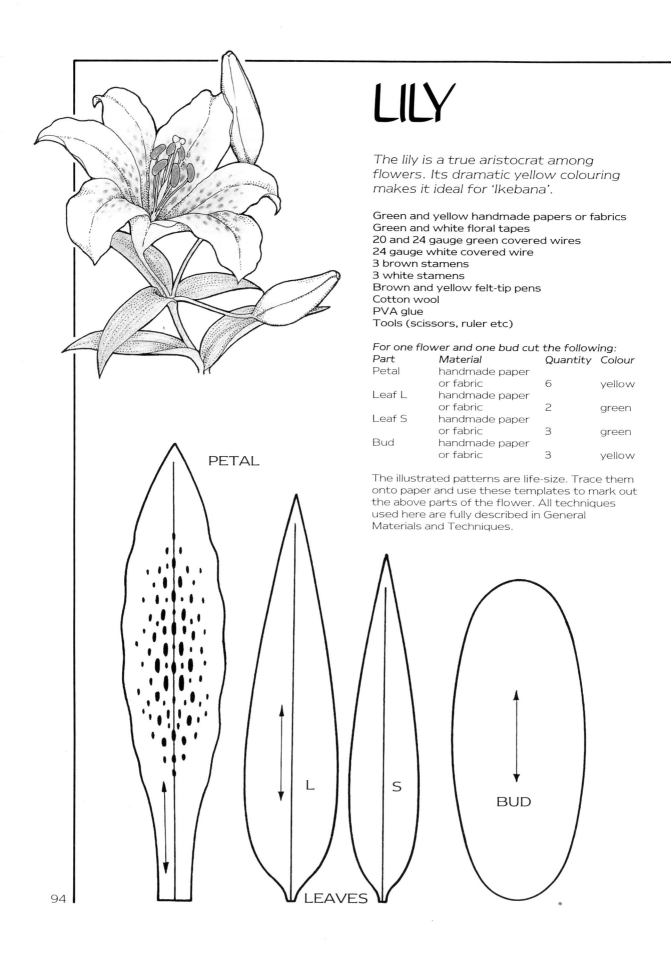

PETAL

LEAVES

L

S

BUD

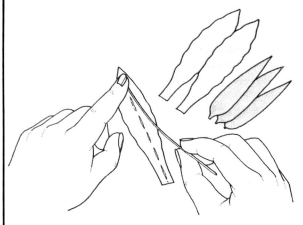

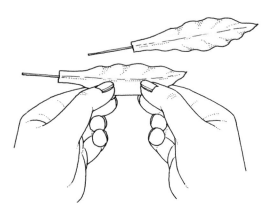

1 Cut six 15cm (6in) lengths of 24 gauge white covered wire and colour them in with the yellow felt-tip pen. Glue a length of yellow wire onto each petal.

2 When their lengths of wire are firmly glued into place, flute each petal.

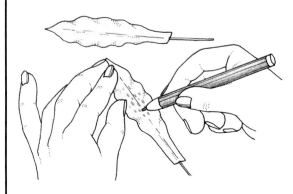

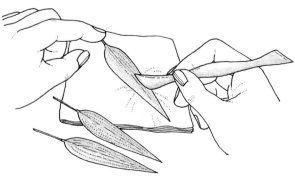

3 With their wired side facing downwards, speckle each petal with the brown felt-tip pen as illustrated.

4 Glue a 12cm (4½in) length of 24 gauge green covered wire onto each leaf. Emboss each leaf.

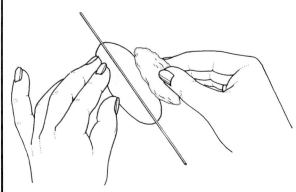

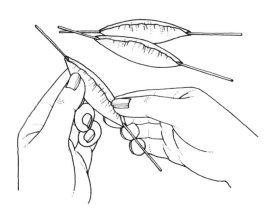

BUD

5 Cut a 15cm (6in) length of 24 gauge white covered wire and place it onto one bud, so that it protrudes equally from either end. Place one good brazil-nut-sized piece of cotton wool on top of the wire.

6 Wrap the bud around the wire and cotton wool, so that its sides overlap slightly. Glue the overlapping sides together, making a cocoon-shaped bud. Repeat steps 5 and 6 with the remaining buds.

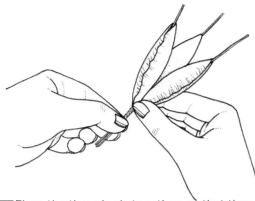

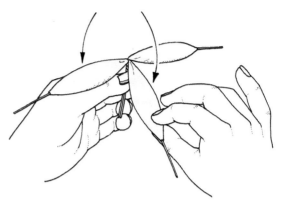

7 Place the three buds together, so that they are of equal height and their glued sides are facing outwards. Twist together the buds' bottom wires and, at the same time, take in a tiny fraction of their bases.

8 Hold the twisted wires in one hand and, with the other, bend the buds outwards and down at their joint. Continue bending the buds down . . .

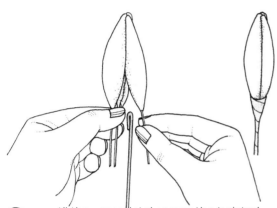

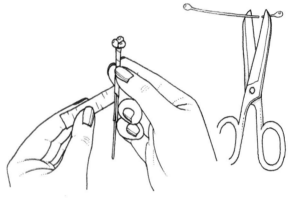

9 . . . until they completely cover the twisted wires and their glued sides are facing inwards. Cut a 15cm (6in) length of 20 gauge wire and bend a small hook into one end. Insert the hook between the buds. Fasten the buds, at their bases, onto the hooked wire with green tape. Continue taping to the end of the wire. Bend the bud's head over a little at its base.

FLOWER

10 From each of the three white stamens cut off and discard a single head. With their heads at the same height, fasten the stamens together with white tape.

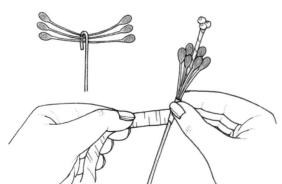

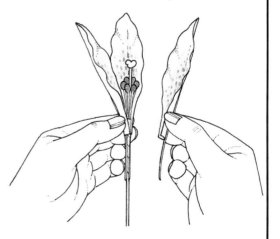

11 Make one flower centre consisting of a 15cm (6in) length of 20 gauge wire and the three brown stamens. Making sure that the white stamens protrude 1cm (½in) above the flower centre, fasten them together, at their bases, with green tape.

12 With their wired side facing outwards, tape three petals, at their bases, around the flower centre.

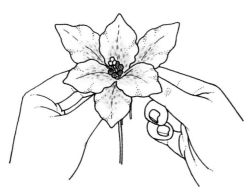

13 With their wired side facing outwards, place the remaining petals over the spaces between the previous ones.

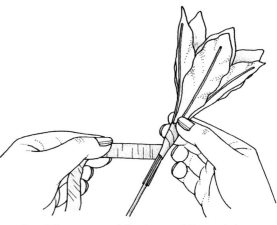

14 Tape around the base of the petals, so fastening them onto the stem. Continue taping to the end of the stem.

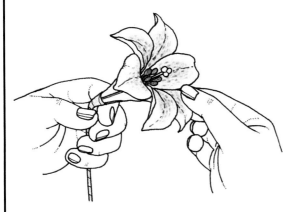

15 At the bottom of its base, gently bend the flower head over. Trying not to open the lily out completely, and keeping its trumpet-like shape, gently curl the petals, one by one.

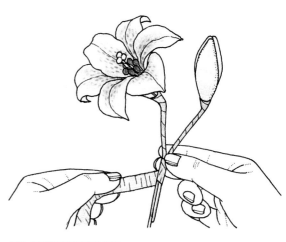

TO JOIN TOGETHER

16 At about 7cm (3in) down from their bases tape the bud and flower together. Continue taping . . .

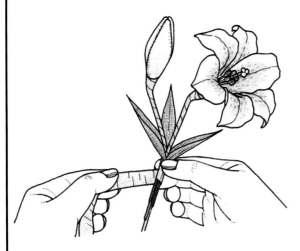

17 . . . and, to hide the joint where the two stems meet, add on leaves S. Continue taping . . .

18 . . . and, about 2cm (¾in) below leaves S, add on leaves L. Continue taping to the end of the stem. Arrange to look lifelike.

BOUVARDIA

The small, pretty bouvardia is an ideal supplementary flower for any arrangement or bouquet.

Green and white handmade papers or fabrics
Green and white floral tapes
20 and 24 gauge wires
5 white stamens
PVA glue
Tools (scissors, ruler etc)

For one group of bouvardia flowers cut the following:

Part	Material	Quantity	Colour
Petal	handmade paper or fabric	5	white
Bud	handmade paper or fabric	3	white
Calyx	handmade paper or fabric	1	green
Corolla	handmade paper or fabric	8	white

The illustrated patterns are life-size. Trace them onto paper and use these templates to mark out the above parts of the flower. All techniques used here are fully described in General Materials and Techniques.

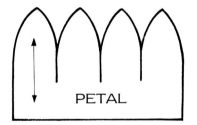

PETAL

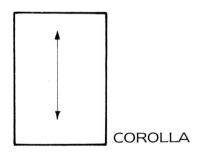

COROLLA

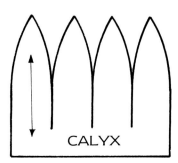

CALYX

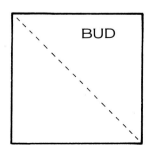

BUD

BOUVARDIA

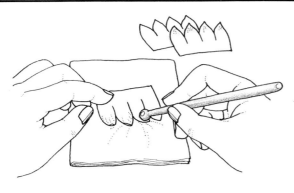

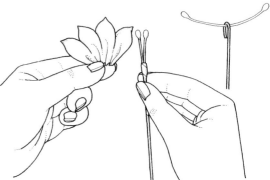

FLOWER

1 Cup the tips of each petal.

2 Make one flower centre consisting of an 8cm (3in) length of 24 gauge wire, one stamen and a length of white tape. Make small, even gathers along one petal's bottom edge, making it fan-like in appearance. Making sure that the petal's cupped side is facing outwards, place the flower centre onto it.

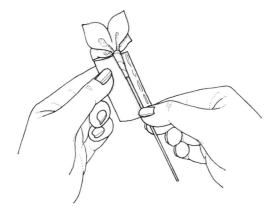

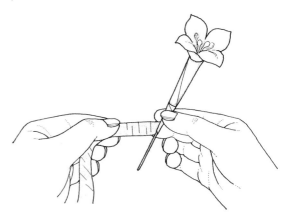

3 Wrap the petal around the flower centre, so that its sides overlap slightly. Fasten the petal, at its base, onto the stem with white tape. Starting at the petal's base, glue one corolla lengthways around the stem.

4 Fasten the corolla, at its base, onto the stem with green tape. Repeat steps 2 to 4 with the remaining petals.

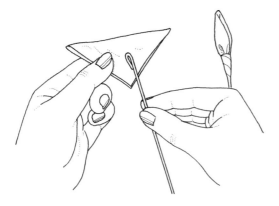

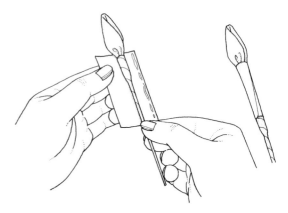

BUD

5 Make one bud consisting of an 8cm (3in) length of 24 gauge wire, one bud and a length of white tape.

6 Starting at the bud's base, glue one corolla lengthways around the stem. Fasten the corolla, at its base, onto the stem with green tape. Repeat steps 5 and 6 with the remaining buds.

7 Cut a 20cm (8in) length of 20 gauge wire and bend a small hook into one end. Arrange all the buds and flowers so that their tops are at the same height. Fasten the arrangement together with a little tape. Hook the wire into the arrangement. Continue taping, fastening the arrangement and hooked wire together.

8 Tape the calyx, at its base, around the joint where all the stems meet. Continue taping to the end of the stem. Carefully bend all the buds and flowers outwards a little, to make the bouvardia look lifelike.

FLOWERS FOR A BOUQUET

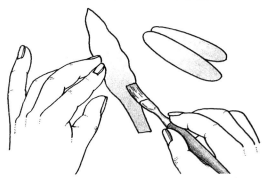

For the bouquet in the photograph you will need 6 lilies, 7 lily buds, 7 lily leaves and 8 bouvardia groups. Full instructions for assembling and finishing the bouquet are given in Assembling the Bridal Bouquet and Corsage.

1 Make the lilies and their buds out of white velvet fabric. For a more natural appearance use the gradation dyeing technique and dye each of the petals and buds on their velvet side. The ideal colouring, from top to bottom, should be white gradually passing through to light green.

BOUQUET
2 From about 12cm (4½in) below their bases, fasten together the six lilies and five bouvardia groups with green tape.

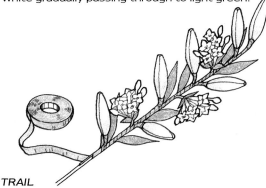

TRAIL
3 Onto a fairly long length of 20 gauge wire, arrange the buds, leaves and the remaining bouvardia groups and fasten together with green tape.

4 Fasten the bouquet and trail together with white tape. You may have to bend the trail a little, so that it can be taped into place. Continue taping to the end of the stem, to make a handle.

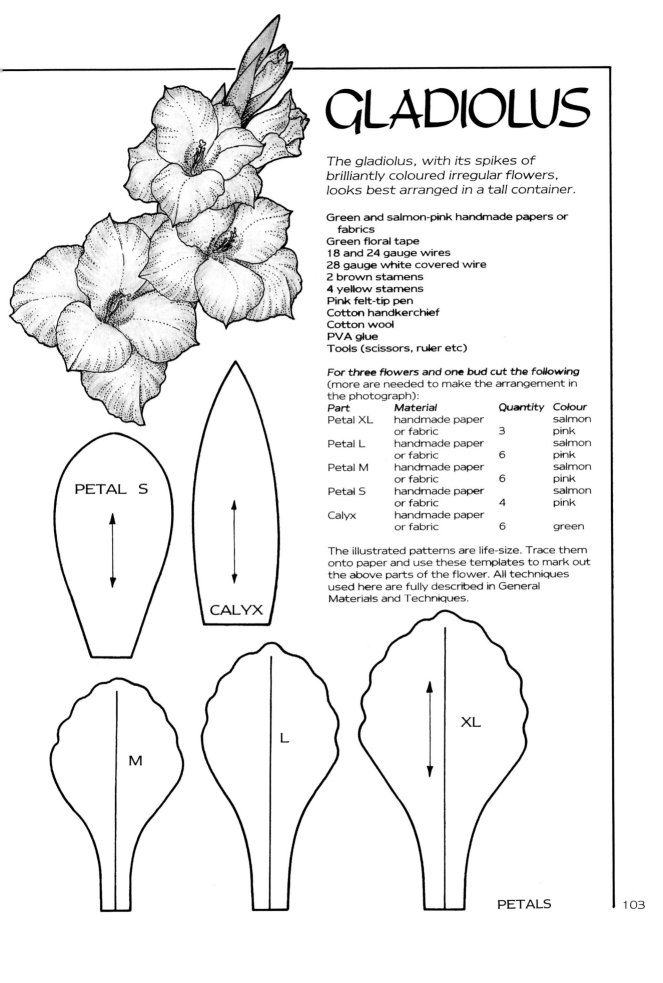

GLADIOLUS

The gladiolus, with its spikes of brilliantly coloured irregular flowers, looks best arranged in a tall container.

Green and salmon-pink handmade papers or fabrics
Green floral tape
18 and 24 gauge wires
28 gauge white covered wire
2 brown stamens
4 yellow stamens
Pink felt-tip pen
Cotton handkerchief
Cotton wool
PVA glue
Tools (scissors, ruler etc)

For three flowers and one bud cut the following (more are needed to make the arrangement in the photograph):

Part	Material	Quantity	Colour
Petal XL	handmade paper or fabric	3	salmon pink
Petal L	handmade paper or fabric	6	salmon pink
Petal M	handmade paper or fabric	6	salmon pink
Petal S	handmade paper or fabric	4	salmon pink
Calyx	handmade paper or fabric	6	green

The illustrated patterns are life-size. Trace them onto paper and use these templates to mark out the above parts of the flower. All techniques used here are fully described in General Materials and Techniques.

PETAL S

CALYX

M

L

XL

PETALS

GLADIOLUS

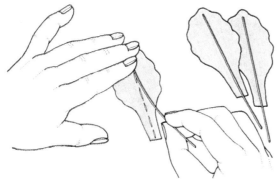
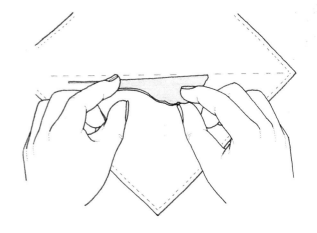

PETALS

1 Cut the following lengths of 28 gauge white covered wire: for petals M six 8cm (3in) lengths, for petals L six 9cm (3½in) lengths and for petals XL three 10cm (4in) lengths. Colour the lengths of wire in with the pink felt-tip pen. Glue the lengths of pink wire onto their respective petals.

2 When their lengths of wire are firmly glued into place, crinkle each petal and also each calyx.

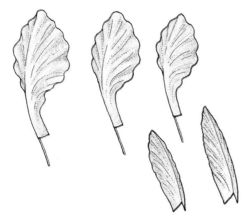
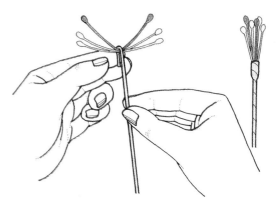

3 Keeping their cup-like shape, gently open out each petal and calyx.

4 Make two flower centres, each one consisting of an 8cm (3in) length of 24 gauge wire, two yellow stamens, one brown stamen and a length of tape.

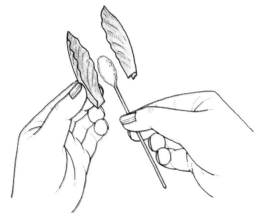

BUD

5 Make one little fingertip-sized pompon consisting of an 8cm (3in) length of 20 gauge wire and a little cotton wool. With their cupped side facing inwards, tape two petals S around the pompon, making a closed bud.

6 Place one calyx around the bud's base. Tape around the calyx's base, fastening it onto the stem. Continue taping to the end of the stem.

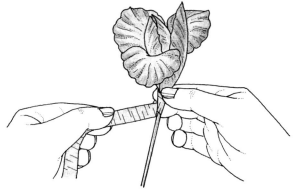

SMALL FLOWER

7 Repeat step 5, so making another bud. With their wired side facing outwards, place petals M around the bud. Tape around the base of the petals, so fastening them onto the stem.

8 Place one calyx around the base of the petals. Tape around the calyx's base, fastening it onto the stem. Continue taping to the end of the stem.

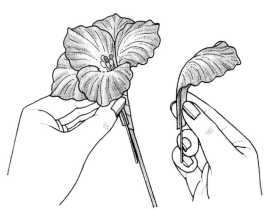

MEDIUM FLOWER

9 With their wired side facing outwards, place the remaining petals M around one flower centre. Tape around the base of the petals, so fastening them onto the stem.

10 With their wired side facing outwards place three petals L over the spaces between petals M. Put a little tape around the base of the petals.

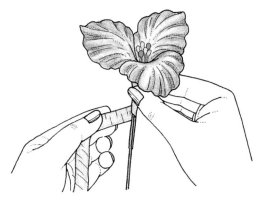

11 Place one calyx around the base of the petals. Tape around the calyx's base, fastening it and petals L onto the stem. Continue taping to the end of the stem.

LARGE FLOWER

12 With their wired side facing outwards, place the remaining petals L around the remaining flower centre. Tape around the base of the petals, fastening them onto the stem.

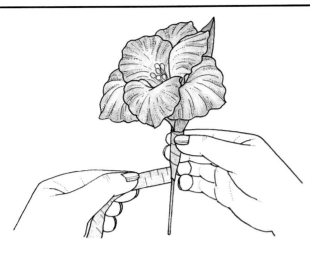

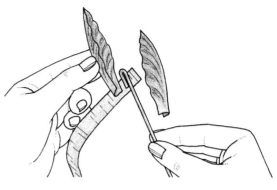

13 With their wired side facing outwards, place petals XL over the spaces between petals L. Place one calyx around the base of the petals. Tape around the calyx's base, fastening it and petals XL onto the stem. Continue taping to the end of the stem.

TO JOIN TOGETHER

14 Cut a fairly long length of 18 gauge wire and bend a small hook into one end. Making sure that their cupped side is facing inwards, tape the remaining calyxes around the hook, one slightly below the other. Continue taping . . .

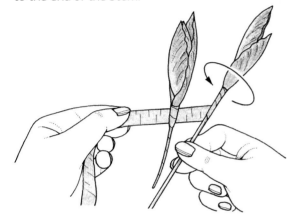

15 . . . and, about 3cm (1¼in) down from the base of the calyxes, add on the bud, so that its calyx is next to the stem. Continue taping . . .

16 . . . and, about 3cm (1¼in) down from the bud's base, add on the small flower, so that its calyx is next to the stem. Continue taping . . .

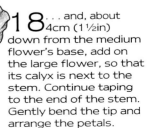

17 . . . and, about 4cm (1½in) down from the small flower's base, add on the medium flower, so that its calyx is next to the stem. Continue taping . . .

18 . . . and, about 4cm (1½in) down from the medium flower's base, add on the large flower, so that its calyx is next to the stem. Continue taping to the end of the stem. Gently bend the tip and arrange the petals.

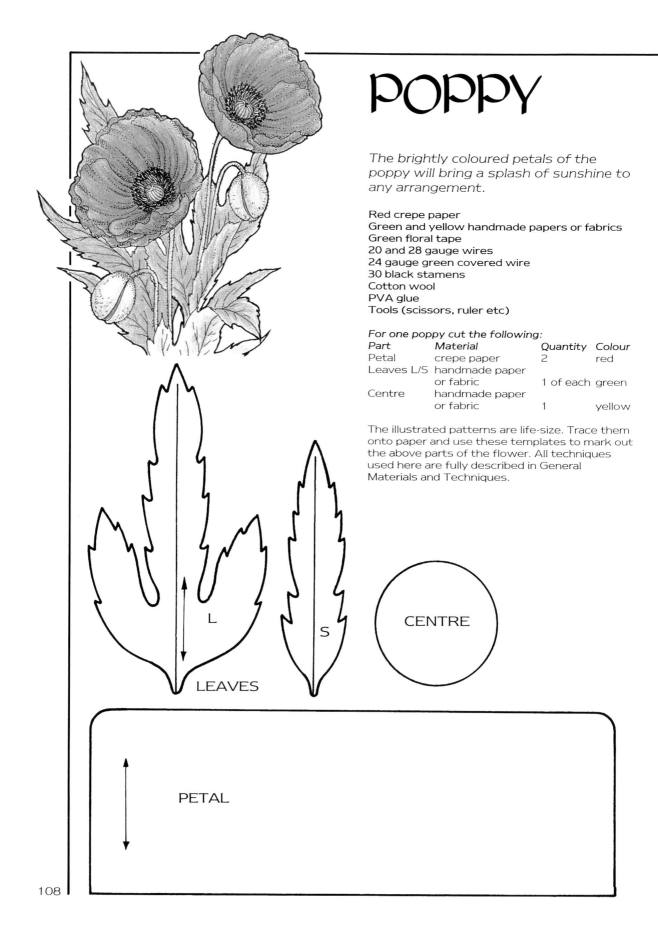

POPPY

The brightly coloured petals of the poppy will bring a splash of sunshine to any arrangement.

Red crepe paper
Green and yellow handmade papers or fabrics
Green floral tape
20 and 28 gauge wires
24 gauge green covered wire
30 black stamens
Cotton wool
PVA glue
Tools (scissors, ruler etc)

For one poppy cut the following:

Part	Material	Quantity	Colour
Petal	crepe paper	2	red
Leaves L/S	handmade paper or fabric	1 of each	green
Centre	handmade paper or fabric	1	yellow

The illustrated patterns are life-size. Trace them onto paper and use these templates to mark out the above parts of the flower. All techniques used here are fully described in General Materials and Techniques.

L

S

LEAVES

CENTRE

PETAL

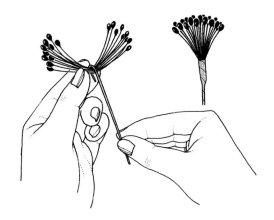

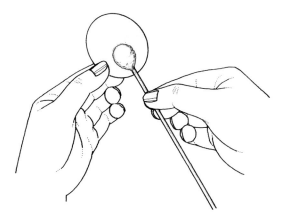

1 Make three flower centres, each one consisting of a 5cm (2in) length of 28 gauge wire, ten black stamens and a length of tape.

CENTRE BALL

2 Make one little fingertip-sized pompon consisting of a 20cm (8in) length of 20 gauge wire and a little cotton wool. Completely cover the pompon with the centre. Tape around the centre's base, so fastening it onto the stem.

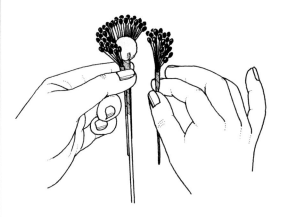

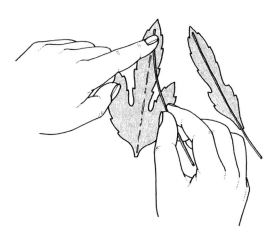

3 Place the three flower centres around the centre ball's base. Tape the flower centres, at their bases, onto the stem.

4 Glue a 10cm (4in) length of 24 gauge green covered wire onto each leaf.

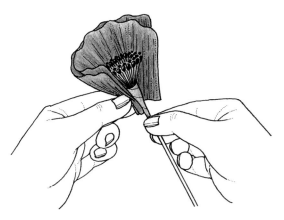

FLOWER

5 Place the two petals on top of each other. Hold the petals together as one and make small, even gathers along their bottom edges, making them fan-like.

6 Wrap the petals around the flower centre, so that their sides overlap slightly.

POPPY

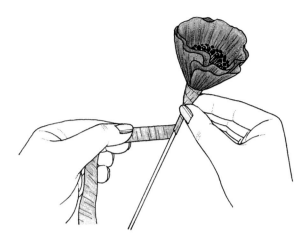

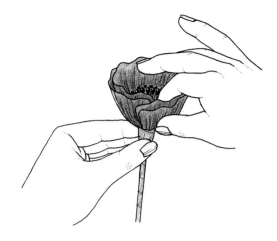

7 Tape around the base of the petals, fastening them onto the stem. Continue taping a further 9cm (3½in) along the stem.

8 Gently open out the flower, to make it bell-like.

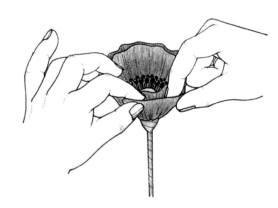

9 Being careful not to tear the paper, frill the entire length of the flower's top edges.

10 About 8cm (3in) below the flower's base, tape leaf S onto the stem. Continue taping . . .

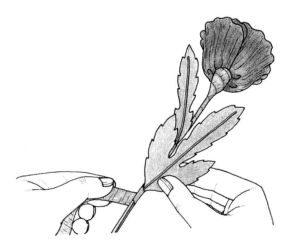

11 . . . and, about 4cm (1½in) below leaf S, add on leaf L. Continue taping to the end of the stem.

12 Gently arrange the leaves, to make the poppy look lifelike.

COSMOS

This showy pink, yellow and green flower comes from the tropics.

Green, light-green, pink and yellow handmade papers or fabrics
Green floral tape
20 gauge wire
24 gauge green covered wire
Cotton wool
PVA glue
Tools (scissors, ruler etc)

For one bud and two flowers cut the following:

Part	Material	Quantity	Colour
Petals L/S	handmade paper or fabric	1 of each	pink
Leaf	handmade paper or fabric	4	green
Bud	handmade paper or fabric	1	pink
Calyx	handmade paper or fabric	3	green
Stamen A	handmade paper or fabric	2	light green
Stamen B	handmade paper or fabric	2	yellow

The illustrated patterns are life-size. Trace them onto paper and use these templates to mark out the above parts of the flower. All techniques used here are fully described in General Materials and Techniques.

STAMEN A

STAMEN B

BUD

LEAF

CALYX

L
S PETALS

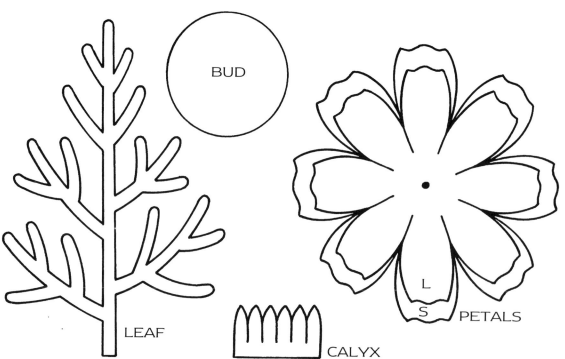

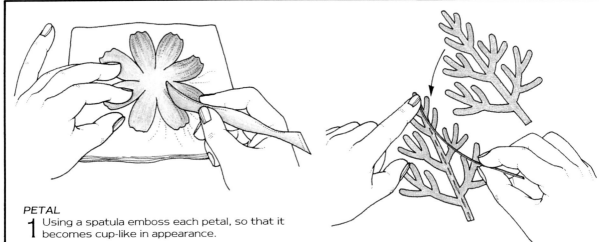

PETAL

1 Using a spatula emboss each petal, so that it becomes cup-like in appearance.

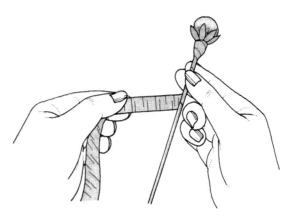

LEAVES

2 Glue a 10cm (4in) length of 24 gauge green covered wire onto two of the leaves. Over the top of each wired leaf glue another leaf, so the length of wire is sandwiched between them.

BUD

3 Make one little fingertip-sized pompon consisting of a 10cm (4in) length of 20 gauge wire and a little cotton wool. Completely cover the pompon with the bud. Tape around the bud's base, fastening it onto the stem.

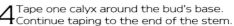

4 Tape one calyx around the bud's base. Continue taping to the end of the stem.

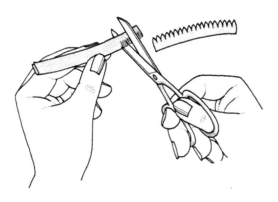

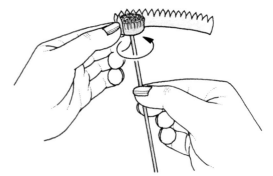

SMALL FLOWER

5 Fold one stamen A in half lengthways and cut a tiny fringe along its folded edge. Be careful not to cut right through to the open edge. Serrate one stamen B as illustrated.

6 Cut a 10cm (4in) length of 20 gauge wire and bend a small hook into one end. Spread a little glue along the bottom edge of one stamen A and hook the wire into one end. Roll the stamen tightly around the wire. Fasten its end with a little glue. Roll, with its V-shaped teeth pointing upwards, stamen B around stamen A. Fasten its end with a little glue.

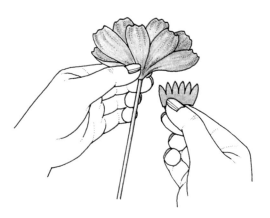

7 With petal S's cupped side facing upwards, place a little glue around its centre. Pass the stamen's wire through the petal's centre, so gluing the stamen onto the petal.

8 Tape one calyx around the petal's base. Continue taping . . .

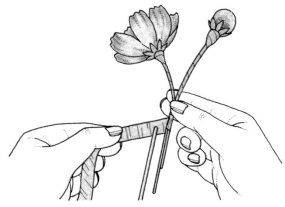

9 . . . to the end of the stem. Finally arrange the petals of the small flower. Making sure that its cupped side is facing downwards, repeat steps 5 to 9 with petal L, so making a large flower.

TO JOIN TOGETHER

10 About 4cm (1½in) down from their bases, tape the small flower and bud onto a length of 20 gauge wire. Continue taping . . .

11 . . . and, about 3cm (1¼in) down from the joint where the small flower and bud meet, add on the two leaves. Continue taping . . .

12 . . . and, about 2cm (¾in) down from the leaves, add on the large flower. Continue taping to the end of the stem. Arrange gently.

NERINE

The dainty pink, strap-shaped petals of the nerine look most attractive when the flower is arranged in a simple container.

Green and pink handmade paper or fabrics
Green floral tape
20 and 30 gauge wires
24 gauge green covered wire
28 gauge white covered wire
12 pink stamens
Pink felt-tip pen
PVA glue
Tools (scissors, ruler etc)

For one group of nerine cut the following:

Part	Material	Quantity	Colour
Petal	handmade paper or fabric	24	pink
Calyx	handmade paper or fabric	4	green

The illustrated patterns are life-size. Trace them onto paper and use these templates to mark out the above parts of the flower. All techniques used here are fully described in General Materials and Techniques.

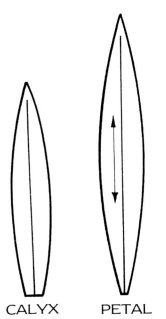

CALYX   PETAL

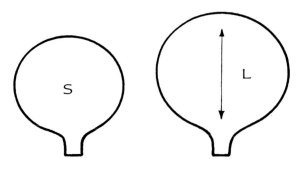

EUCALYPTUS LEAVES

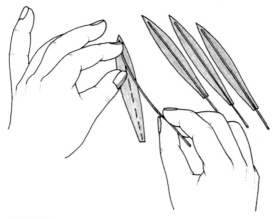

PETALS

1 Cut twenty-four 9cm (3½in) lengths of 28 gauge white covered wire and colour them in with the pink felt-tip pen. Glue a length of pink wire onto each petal.

2 When their lengths of wire are firmly glued into place, flute each petal.

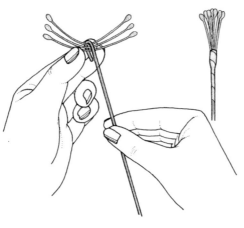

3 Make four flower centres, each one consisting of a 13cm (5in) length of 24 gauge wire, three pink stamens and a length of tape.

4 With their wired side facing outwards, place six petals around one flower centre.

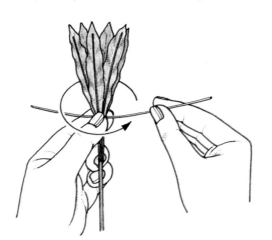

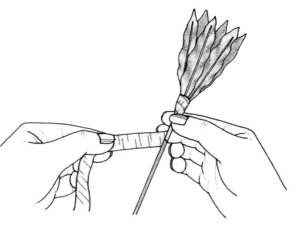

5 Bind a short length of 30 gauge wire around the base of the petals, so fastening them onto the stem.

6 Cover the binding with a length of tape. Continue taping to the end of the stem.

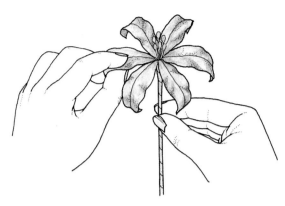

7 Gently curl the petals backwards, so giving the nerine its characteristic shape. Repeat steps 4 to 7 with the remaining petals.

TO JOIN TOGETHER
8 Cut a fairly long length of 20 gauge wire and bend a small hook into one end. About 7cm (3in) down from their bases, tape two flowers together and hook the wire between them. Tape the flowers and hooked wire together.

9 At the point where the previous flowers are joined, tape the remaining flowers onto the stem, about 7cm (3in) down from their bases. You will have to bend the stem of each flower over a little, so that it can be taped into place.

10 Glue a 7cm (3in) length of 24 gauge green covered wire onto each calyx. With their wired side facing outwards, tape the calyxes, at their bases, around the joint. Continue taping to the end of the stem.

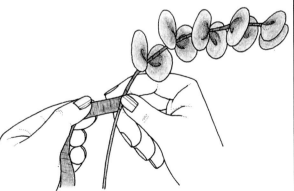

FINISHING OFF
11 Carefully arrange the flowers into a ball-like shape, to make the nerine look lifelike.

12 As in the photograph, try arranging the nerine with some sprays of eucalyptus coloured to match.

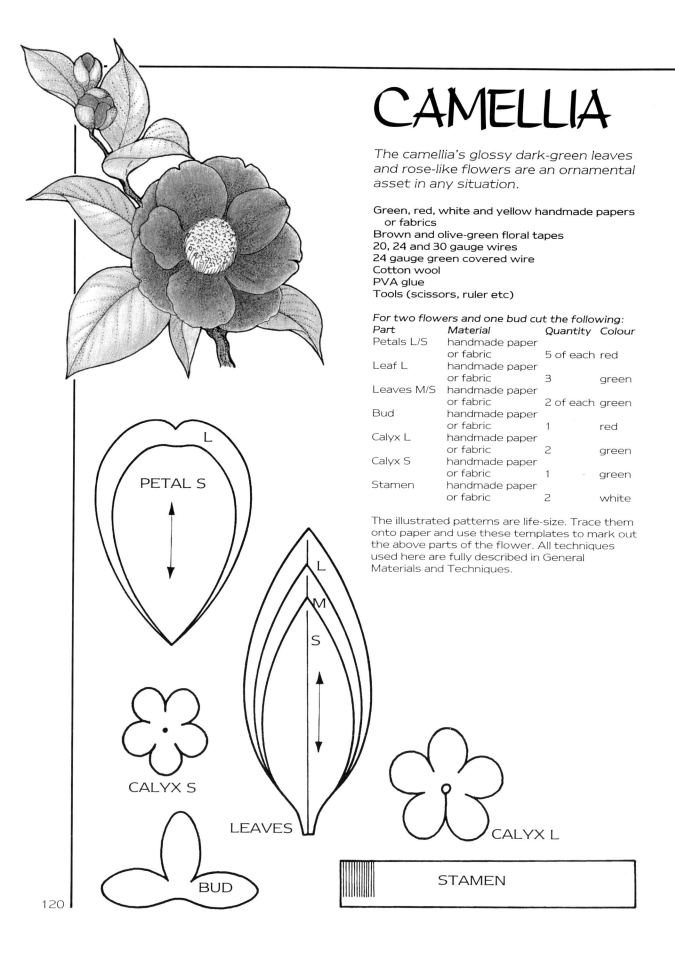

CAMELLIA

The camellia's glossy dark-green leaves and rose-like flowers are an ornamental asset in any situation.

Green, red, white and yellow handmade papers
   or fabrics
Brown and olive-green floral tapes
20, 24 and 30 gauge wires
24 gauge green covered wire
Cotton wool
PVA glue
Tools (scissors, ruler etc)

For two flowers and one bud cut the following:

Part	Material	Quantity	Colour
Petals L/S	handmade paper or fabric	5 of each	red
Leaf L	handmade paper or fabric	3	green
Leaves M/S	handmade paper or fabric	2 of each	green
Bud	handmade paper or fabric	1	red
Calyx L	handmade paper or fabric	2	green
Calyx S	handmade paper or fabric	1	green
Stamen	handmade paper or fabric	2	white

The illustrated patterns are life-size. Trace them onto paper and use these templates to mark out the above parts of the flower. All techniques used here are fully described in General Materials and Techniques.

PETAL S
L

CALYX S

LEAVES
L
M
S

CALYX L

BUD

STAMEN

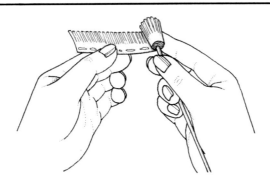

STAMEN

1 Cut a 10cm (4in) length of 24 gauge wire and bend a small hook into one end. Cut a very fine fringe all the way round one stamen's top edge. Spread a little glue along the stamen's bottom edge and hook the wire into one end. Roll the stamen tightly around the wire. Fasten the end with a little glue.

2 Cut a small piece of the yellow material into very fine flakes. Cover the stamen's head with glue and dip it into the flakes. Repeat steps 1 and 2 with the remaining stamen.

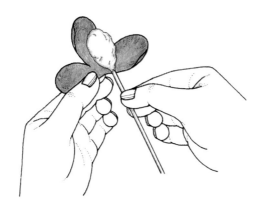

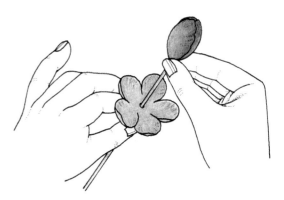

BUD

3 Make one little fingertip-sized pompon consisting of a 10cm (4in) length of 20 gauge wire and a little cotton wool. With the aid of a little glue wrap the pompon inside the bud's petals.

4 Pass the bud's wire through calyx S's centre.

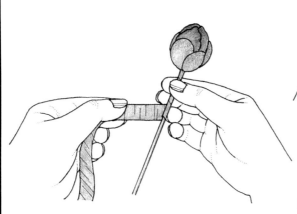

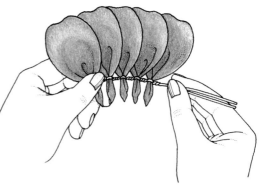

5 With the aid of a little glue wrap the calyx around the bud. Starting adjacent to the calyx, cover the stem all the way to the end with olive-green tape.

6 Small flower — repeat steps 4 to 6 of the rose with petals S (p130).

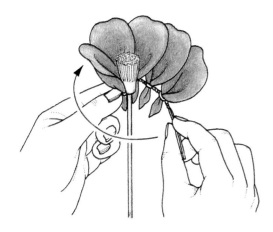

7 With their cupped side facing inwards wrap petals S around the stamen. Bind the excess wire around the base of the petals, fastening them onto the stem.

8 Tape around the binding, hiding it. Glue calyx L around the flower's bottom. Continue taping to the end of the stem.

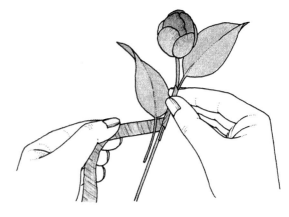

LARGE FLOWER

9 Repeat steps 6 to 8 with petal L and the remaining stamen.

TO JOIN TOGETHER

10 Glue a 9cm (3½in) length of 24 gauge green covered wire onto each leaf. With brown tape fasten the bud and one leaf S together. Continue taping . . .

11 . . . and add on the remaining leaf S, and leaves M, each about 2cm (¾in) apart, the small flower . . .

12 . . . leaves L and the large flower. Continue taping to the end of the stem.

CYCLAMEN

The showy, drooping flowers and heart-shaped leaves of the cyclamen make it a perennial favourite.

Green and pink handmade papers or fabrics
Brown and olive-green floral tapes
20 gauge wire
28 gauge white covered wire
Small flowerpot filled with oasis
Pink felt-tip pen
Cotton wool
PVA glue
Tools (scissors, ruler etc)

For one plant cut the following:

Part	Material	Quantity	Colour
Petal	handmade paper or fabric	12	pink
Leaves L/M/S	handmade paper or fabric	3 of each	green
Bud	handmade paper or fabric	2	pink

The illustrated patterns are life-size. Trace them onto paper and use these templates to mark out the above parts of the flower. All techniques used here are fully described in General Materials and Techniques.

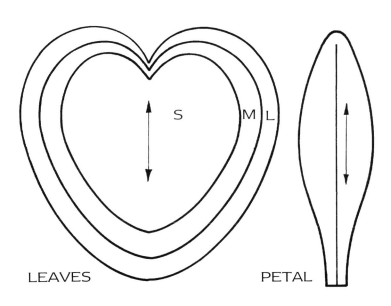

S M L

LEAVES

PETAL

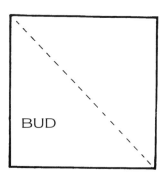

BUD

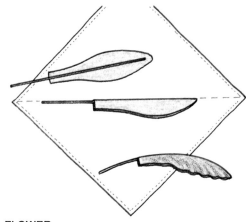

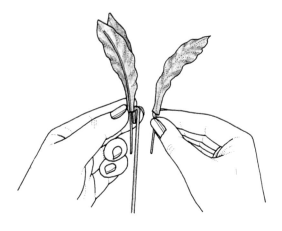

FLOWER

1 Cut twelve 9cm (3½in) lengths of 28 gauge white covered wire and colour them in with the pink felt-tip pen. Glue a length of pink wire onto each petal. Crinkle each petal.

2 Cut a 15cm (6in) length of 20 gauge wire and bend a small hook into one end. With their wired side facing outwards place six of the petals around the hook.

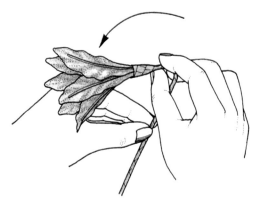

4 Bend the flower over from just below its base.

3 Fasten the petals, at their bases, onto the hooked wire with brown tape. Continue taping to the end of the stem.

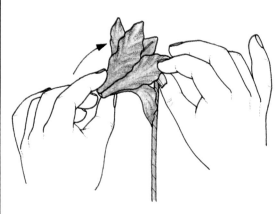

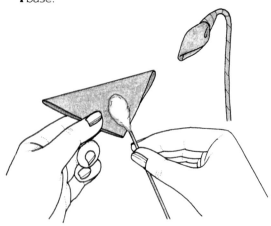

BUD

6 Make two buds, each one consisting of a 10cm (4in) length of 20 gauge wire, an almond-sized pompon, one bud and a length of brown tape. Continue taping to the end of the stems. Bend the buds over, making them cyclamen-like.

5 About 1cm (½in) up from the flower s base turn back the petals, making them cyclamen-like. Repeat steps 2 to 5 with the remaining petals, so making another flower.

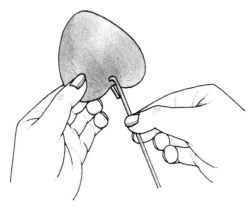
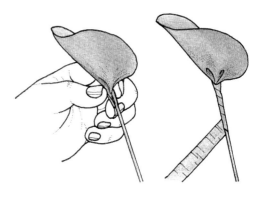

LEAF

7 Cut a 13cm (5in) length of 20 gauge wire and bend a small hook into one end. Hook the wire into the bottom centre of one leaf.

8 Gather the leaf's bottom centre around the hook. Fasten the leaf onto the hooked wire with olive-green tape. Continue taping to the end of the stem. Repeat steps 7 and 8 with the remaining leaves.

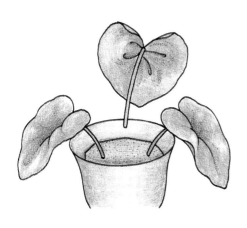
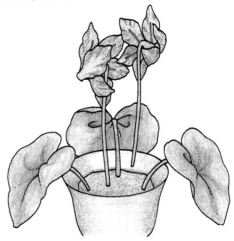

TO BUILD UP THE PLANT

9 Arrange leaves L in the flowerpot's oasis, in a triangular figuration.

10 Arrange the two flowers in the centre of the oasis.

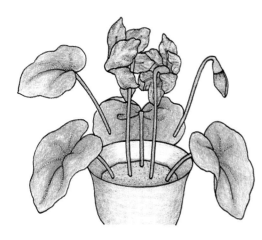
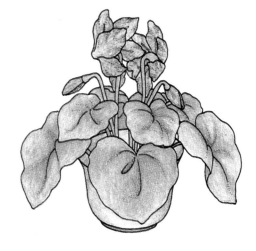

11 Arrange leaves M and S between leaves L. Finally position the buds in the arrangement.

FINISHING OFF

12 Gently arrange the flowers, buds and leaves to make the cyclamen look lifelike.

ROSE

The rose's beauty and elegance add a romantic touch to any gift or arrangement.

Green and red handmade paper or fabrics
Green floral tape
20 and 30 gauge wires
24 gauge green covered wire
Cotton wool
PVA glue
Tools (scissors, ruler etc)

For one large flower cut the following:

Part	Material	Quantity	Colour
Petal L	handmade paper or fabric	5	red
Petal M	handmade paper or fabric	4	red
Petal S	handmade paper or fabric	3	red
Leaf L	handmade paper or fabric	5	green
Leaf S	handmade paper or fabric	3	green
Bud	handmade paper or fabric	1	red
Calyx	handmade paper or fabric	1	green

The illustrated patterns are life-size. Trace them onto paper and use these templates to mark out the above parts of the flower. All techniques used here are fully described in General Materials and Techniques.

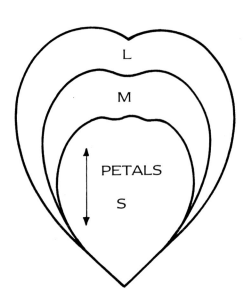

BUD

L

M

PETALS

S

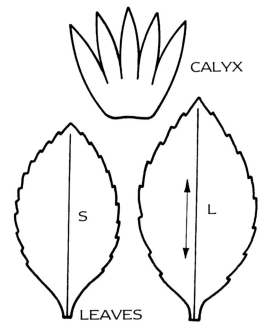

CALYX

S

L

LEAVES

ROSE

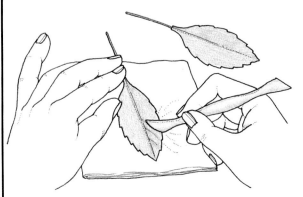

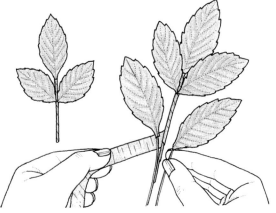

LEAVES

1 Glue a 10cm (4in) length of 24 gauge wire onto each leaf. Emboss each leaf.

2 With the wired side of each leaf facing downwards, tape leaves S into a group. Also tape three leaves L into a group and, about 2cm (¾in) down from their base, tape on the remaining leaves L.

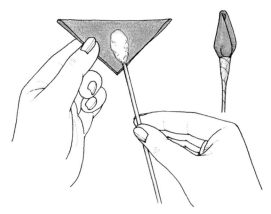

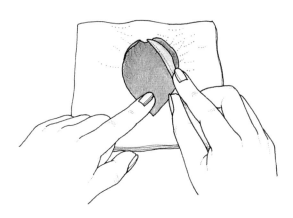

BUD

3 Make one bud consisting of a fairly long length of 20 gauge wire (this is for the rose's stem), a good almond-sized pompon, the bud, and a length of tape.

FLOWER

4 Give a soft forward curl to the top edges of each petal. When completed *turn each petal over*.

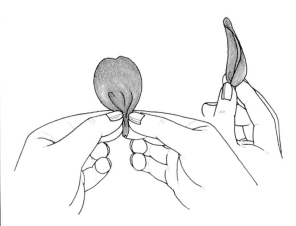

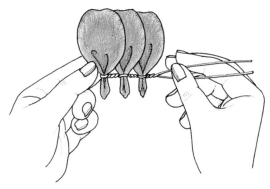

5 Make small, even gathers in each petal's lower edge and cup them so that they resemble the illustration. With their top edges curling outwards . . .

6 . . . group wire petals S together.

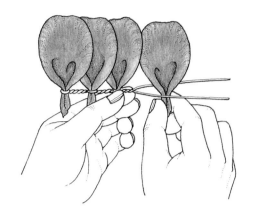

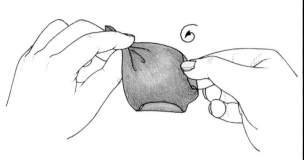

7 Repeat steps 5 and 6 with petals M.

8 Give an extra curl to the upper edges of petals L.

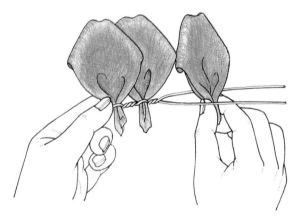

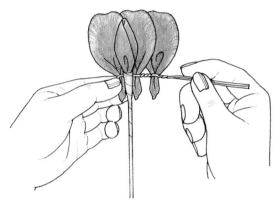

9 Repeat steps 5 and 6 with petals L.

LARGE FLOWER

10 With their cupped side facing inwards wrap petals S around the bud.

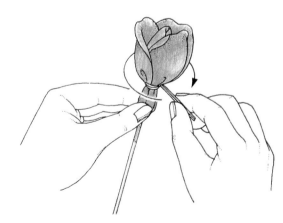

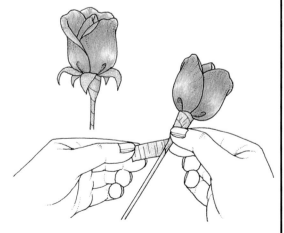

11 Bind the excess wire around the base of the petals, so fastening them onto the stem.

12 Tape around the binding, hiding it. If a small rose is required, then tape the calyx around the flower's base at this stage. To finish off the small rose, add on the groups of leaves S and L (see step 17). Continue taping to the end of the stem.

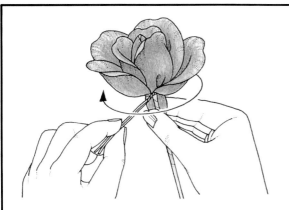

13 With their cupped side facing inwards wrap petals M around petals S. Bind the excess wire around the base of the petals, so fastening them onto the stem.

14 Tape around the binding, hiding it. If a medium-sized rose is required, then tape the calyx around the flower's base at this stage. To finish off the medium rose, add on the groups of leaves S and L (see step 17). Continue taping to the end of the stem.

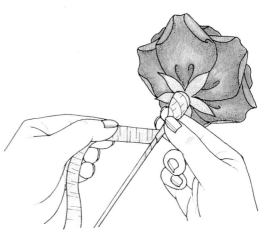

15 With their cupped side facing inwards wrap petals L around petals M. Bind the excess wire around the base of the petals, so fastening them onto the stem.

16 Wrap the calyx around the flower's base. Tape the calyx, at its base, so fastening it onto the stem. Continue taping to the end of the stem.

17 About 10cm (4in) below the flower's base add on the group of leaves S. Continue taping and, a further 5cm (2in) down, add on the group of leaves L. Continue taping to the end of the stem.

FINISHING OFF

18 Arrange the flower and leaves to suit personal taste.

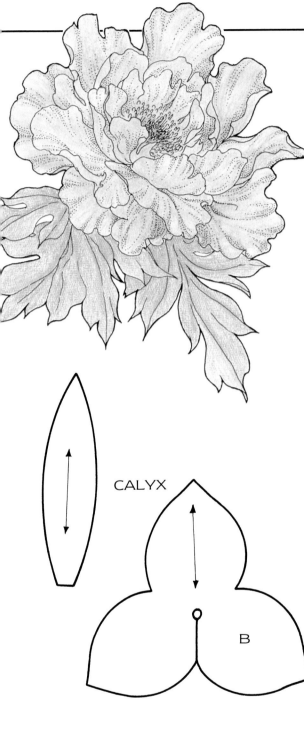

PEONY

The showy and beautiful blossoms of the peony can now be with you all year round.

Green, pink and yellow handmade papers or
    fabrics
Green floral tape
20 gauge wire
24 gauge green covered wire
28 gauge white covered wire
60 yellow stamens
Pink felt-tip pen
Cotton wool
PVA glue
Tools (scissors, ruler etc)

For one flower and bud cut the following:

Part	Material	Quantity	Colour
Petal XL	handmade paper or fabric	5	pink
Petal L	handmade paper or fabric	5	pink
Petal M	handmade paper or fabric	5	pink
Petal S	handmade paper or fabric	13	pink
Leaf L	handmade paper or fabric	1 of each	green
Leaf M	handmade paper or fabric	1	green
Leaf S	handmade paper or fabric	3	green
Calyx A	handmade paper or fabric	3	green
Calyx B	handmade paper or fabric	2	green
Centre	handmade paper or fabric	1	yellow

The illustrated patterns are life-size. Trace them onto paper and use these templates to mark out the above parts of the flower. All techniques used here are fully described in General Materials and Techniques.
    The illustrated patterns for the peony's petals XL and L, leaves L, M and S and the centre can be found overleaf.

CALYX

B

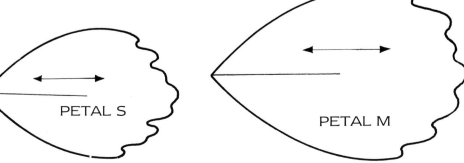

PETAL S

PETAL M

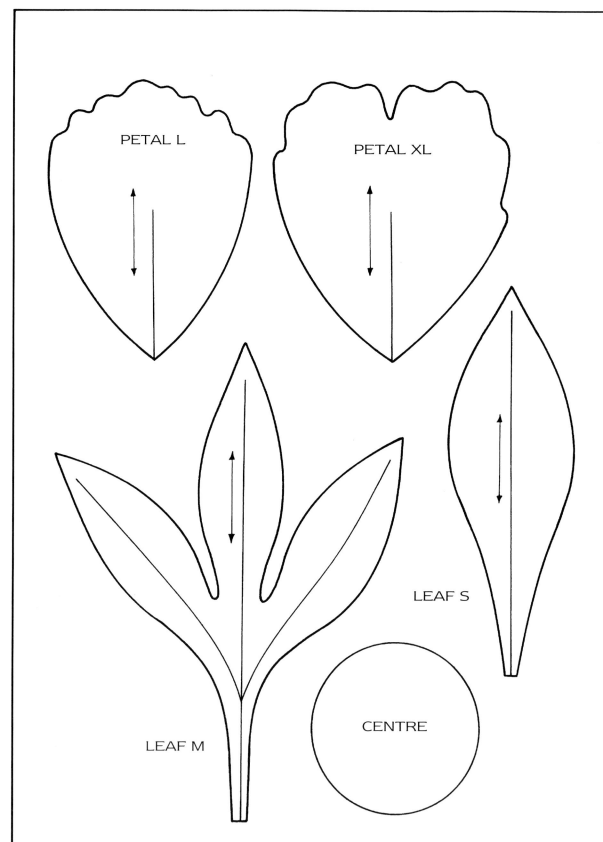

PETAL L

PETAL XL

LEAF S

LEAF M

CENTRE

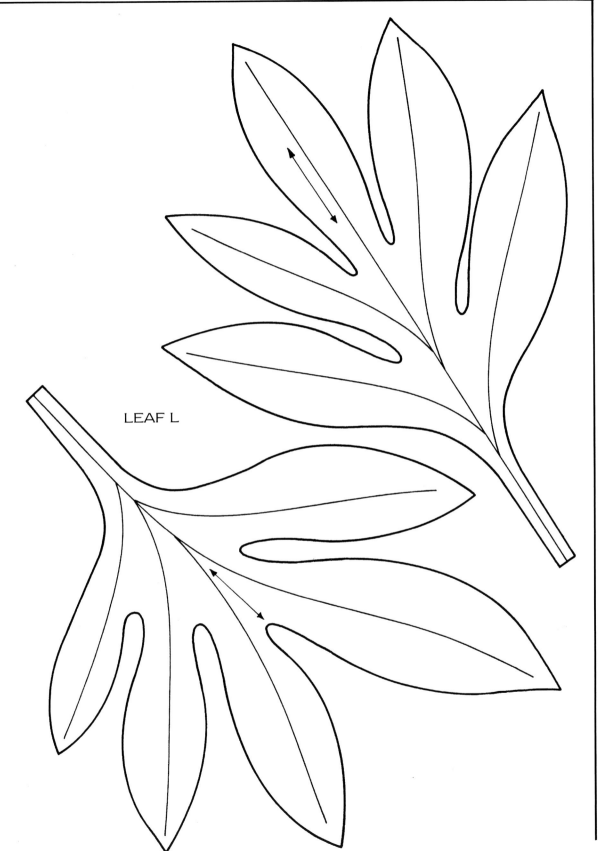

LEAF L

PEONY

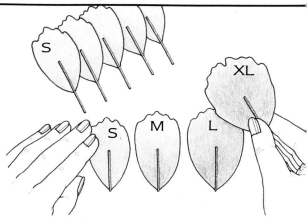

LEAF

1 Cut the required lengths of 24 gauge green covered wire and glue them onto their respective leaves as illustrated.

2 Colour the 28 gauge white covered wire in with the pink felt-tip pen. Cut thirteen 5cm (2in) lengths of pink wire and glue them onto petals S from their middle down. Place three petals S to one side, as later on these will be used for the bud. From another five petals S cut off the protruding wire at their bottom point.

Cut the required lengths of 28 gauge pink-coloured wire and glue them onto their respective petals (XL, L and M) as illustrated.

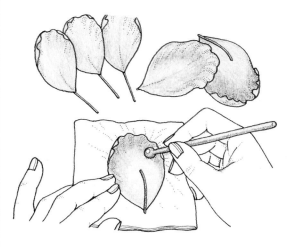

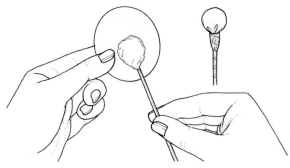

3 With their wired side facing downwards, cup each petal, except the bud's three. Turn petals XL, L and M *only* over and curl their top edge.

CENTRE BALL

4 Make one half-thumbtip-sized pompon consisting of a 15cm (6in) length of 20 gauge wire and a little cotton wool. Completely cover the pompon with the centre. Tape around the centre's base, fastening it onto the stem.

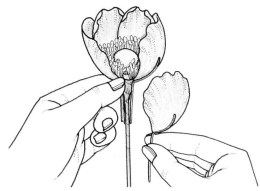

5 Make three flower centres, each one consisting of a 5cm (2in) length of 28 gauge wire, 20 yellow stamens and a length of tape. Tape the flower centres, at their bases, around the centre ball's base.

6 With their cupped side facing inwards, place five petals S (those with protruding wires) around the flower centre. Tape around the protruding wires, so fastening petals S onto the stem.

PEONY

7 With their cupped side facing inwards, place and glue a further five petals S (the ones with no protruding wires) in an alternating pattern to the previous petals S. Make sure that the glue is dry before progressing to the next step.

8 Repeat step 7 with petals M, making sure that they are glued in an alternating pattern to petals S.

9 Repeat step 7 with petals L, making sure that they are glued in an alternating pattern to petals M.

10 Repeat step 7 with petals XL, making sure that they are glued in an alternating pattern to petals L.

11 Glue calyxes A onto the flower's bottom in a triangular figuration. Place one calyx B around the flower's base, in an alternating pattern to calyxes A. Slightly gather calyx B's base, so that it hugs the flower's underside, and glue its tips where they touch.

12 Tape around calyx B's base, so fastening it onto the stem. Continue taping to the end of the stem.

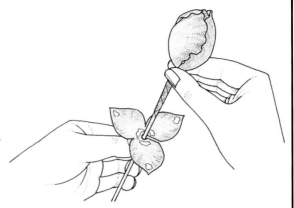

BUD

13 With their wired side facing upwards, cup the three petals S that you placed to one side in step 2. Make one generous thumbtip-sized pompon, consisting of a fairly long length of 20 gauge wire and a little cotton wool. With their cupped side facing inwards wrap petals S around the pompon. Tape around the protruding wires . . .

14 . . . so fastening petals S onto the stem. With the aid of a little glue, wrap the remaining calyx B around the bud.

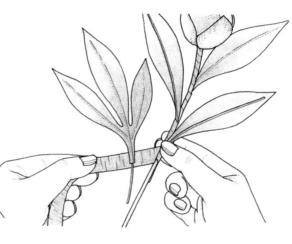

15 Starting adjacent to the bud, cover the stem with tape. About 3cm (1¼in) down from the bud's base, add on leaves S, each about 2cm (¾in) apart . . .

16 . . . and leaf M. Continue taping . . .

17 . . . and, about a further 3cm (1¼in) down, add on the flower and leaves L. Continue taping . . .

18 . . . to the end of the stem. Arrange the peony to suit personal taste.

Dyeing and Sizing

DYEING

Dyes are used to produce the many colour shades and variegated effects which exist in real flowers – thus giving a more accurate reproduction.

Always choose the dye and technique most suitable for the type of material you are using. Before dyeing, soak your material (only handmade paper and fabric) in the liquid permeation solution. Wear rubber gloves and cover your working surface with a layer or two of newspaper. All tools and equipment used here are fully described in Glossary of Tools and Equipment.

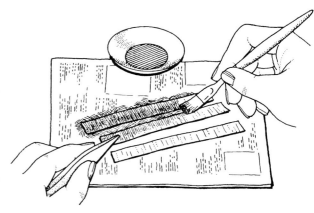

FLORAL TAPE

Cut white floral tape into workable lengths. Using a paintbrush, completely cover the lengths with ink of the required colour. If you ever need brown tape, try dyeing green floral tape with a thin red ink.

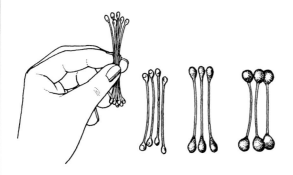

STAMENS

These usually come in a large variety of colours and sizes. If you cannot obtain a specific colour buy white ones and dye with ink. Hold a few stamens (by their middles) using tweezers, and paint them with ink of the required colour. Alternatively, dip the heads only in the ink.

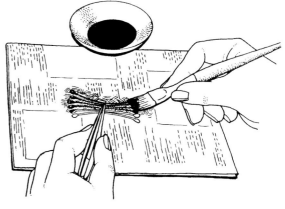

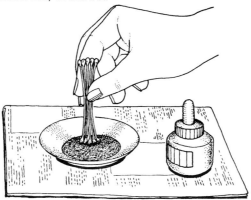

CREPE PAPER

There is a very simple dyeing technique which gives a beautiful gradation effect to crepe paper, helping to make the finished flower more lifelike and natural. Crepe paper can be dyed with ink or direct dye, or try dipping crepe paper into warm water, so releasing its impregnated ink — this solution can then be used as a dye.

2 Wearing rubber gloves, place the required coloured dye on a saucer.

1 Keeping the crepe paper still folded as in the packet, cut it (with due regard to the grain) to the template's height.

3 Dip one end of the crepe paper into the saucer and let it soak up the dye. When the dye is about 1cm (½in) short of the desired depth remove the crepe paper . . .

4 . . . and squeeze out any excess dye.

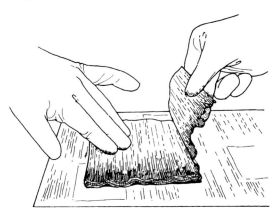

5 Place the dyed crepe paper onto some newspaper. Gently open it out, being careful not to stretch the grain, and leave it to dry.

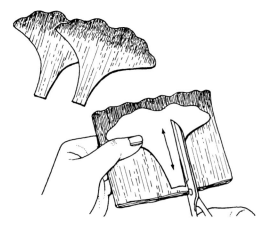

6 When completely dry refold the crepe paper into its original shape, so that it is ready to be cut out.

MIXED COLOURS

Many flowers, like the cyclamen and hydrangea, have a lovely mixed colour to their leaves and petals. This effect is very easily obtained by using ink or direct dye to enrich the original colouring of handmade paper or fabric.

1 Impregnate the material with the liquid permeation solution.

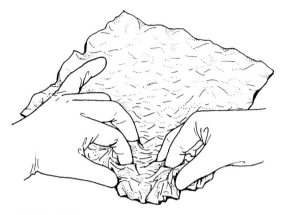

2 Carefully open the material out on a flat surface and crinkle it up, starting from one corner. Make sure that the finished result lies flat and has not become ball-like in shape.

3 Holding the flat shape between your finger-tips (so that it does not open out) dip it into a saucer of dye. Leave it for a few seconds. Gently pick it up, turn it over, and place it into another dye.

4 Again leave it for a few seconds before picking it up. Give it a tight squeeze, causing the colours of the dyes to run together and at the same time removing any excess dye.

5 Gently open out the material, being careful not to tear it.

6 Hang the material up to dry.

FABRIC

The following techniques are used in flower making to give either a gradation of colour or one solid colour (using ink or direct dye). Always make sure that the fabric is sized once the dye is dry.

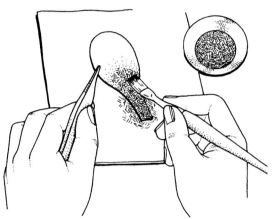

GRADATION

1 Place the previously cut-out petal onto a protective surface (not newspaper). Using a paintbrush, cover it completely with the liquid permeation solution. Let the solution soak through before progressing to the next step.

2 Before the liquid permeation solution is dry, paint the dye on in the required area. As the material is already damp the dye will run, giving the desired effect. Place the petal to one side to dry. Once dry the petal can be sized.

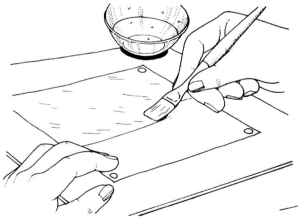

ONE SOLID COLOUR

1 Place the fabric on a piece of board or thick cardboard. Stretch it tightly and secure each corner with a drawing pin. Using a paintbrush, cover it completely with the liquid permeation solution. Let the solution soak through before progressing to the next step.

2 Before the liquid permeation solution is dry, paint all over with dye. Hang the fabric to dry. Once dry the fabric can be sized.

SIZING

Sizing the fabric will prevent the edges of petals, leaves etc from fraying.

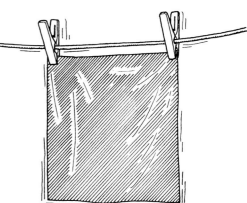

1 Mix a little wallpaper paste and water together as per the instructions on the package. Using a paintbrush, completely cover the fabric with a layer of paste.

2 Carefully remove the fabric from your working surface and hang it up to dry.

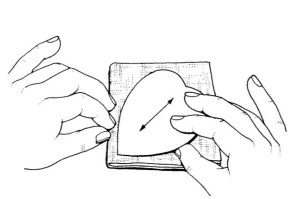

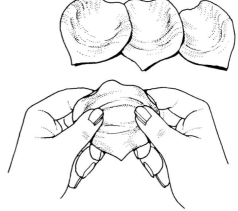

3 Once dry the fabric is ready to be cut out. If you are using a template make sure that the double-headed arrow is pointing along the bias.

4 As it can hold any given shape, sized fabric will help to give body to any part of the flower.

Tips on Petal Cutting

Having to cut out the intricate parts of a petal can be very time consuming. The very easy techniques given below will enable you to cut out various petals with just a few snips of the scissors.

SIX PETALS

This particular technique is ideal for the mass production of Canterbury bell and freesia petals.

Before you start, cut the material into a rectangle that is the same size as the illustrated petal pattern.

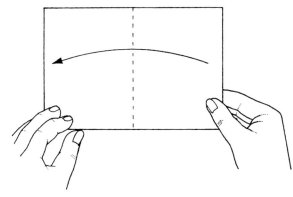

1 Place the rectangle of material before you like a landscape picture and fold it in half from right to left.

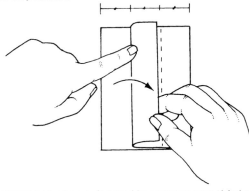

2 Fold the top left-hand layer over one-third of the way towards the right.

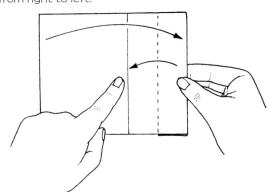

3 Holding the folded third, open out the top layer. Next fold the right-hand folded side over to meet the middle.

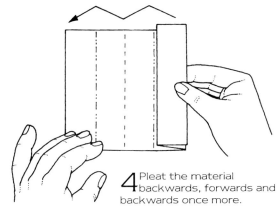

4 Pleat the material backwards, forwards and backwards once more.

5 Cut out the petal's pattern.

6 Carefully open out the material to find the petal. Cut off the excess rectangular sections if the petal has only four or five individual parts to it.

FIVE PETALS

This technique is ideal for the mass production of cherry and strawberry petals.

Before you start, cut the material into a square that is the same size as the illustrated petal pattern.

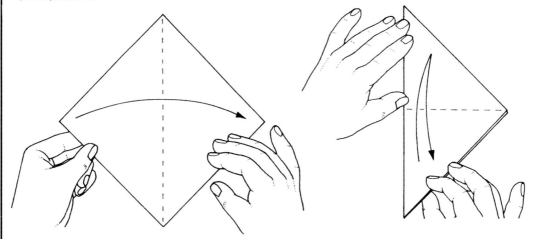

1 Place the square of material before you so that it looks like a diamond and fold it in half from left to right.

2 Fold and unfold it in half from bottom to top.

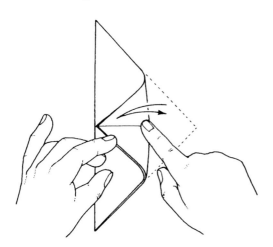

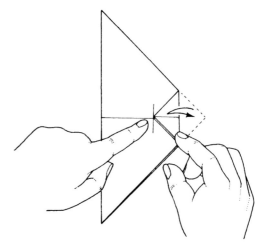

3 Fold the two right-hand corners over to meet the middle of the left-hand side, press them flat in the middle and then unfold.

4 Fold the two right-hand corners over again, this time to meet the crease mark made in step 3. Press them flat and unfold.

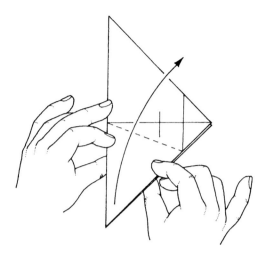

5 From the middle of the left-hand side, fold the bottom point over towards the right. Carefully note where the fold starts and ends . . .

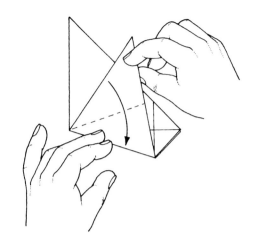

6 . . . then fold it back on itself so it lies straight along the bottom folded edge.

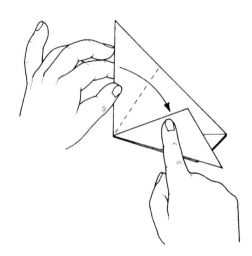

7 As shown, fold the left-hand side over.

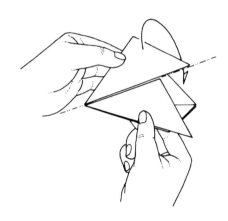

8 Fold in half away from you.

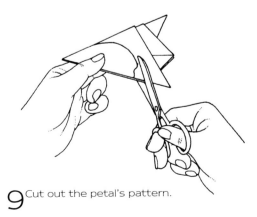

9 Cut out the petal's pattern.

10 Carefully open out the material to find the petal.

147

FOUR PETALS

This technique is ideal for the mass production of hydrangea and carnation petals.

Before you start, cut the material into a square that is the same size as the illustrated petal pattern.

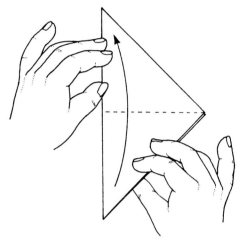

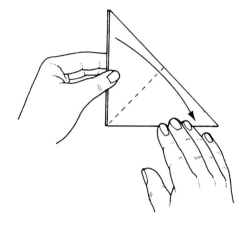

1 Place the square of material before you so that it looks like a diamond and fold it in half from left to right. Next fold it in half from bottom to top.

2 Being careful not to twist the material round, fold the top left-hand points down to meet the bottom right-hand point.

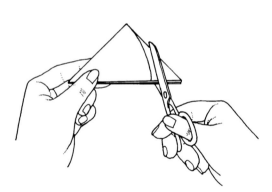

3 At this stage cut out a quarter circle and carefully open out the material to find a carnation petal.

4 Cut out the illustrated pattern and carefully open out the material to find a hydrangea petal.

Assembling a Bridal Bouquet and Corsage

An important part of flower making is deciding what to do with the finished item. Obviously flowers like the cyclamen and strawberry look their 'best' in flower containers, while the lily and bouvardia look most attractive in a bouquet. (See Flowers for a Bouquet, p102.)

28 gauge white covered wire
30 gauge wire
White tape
Lilies, bouvardias and trail (see p102)
White tulle (a net-like material which is used for making veils and dresses and is obtainable from haberdashery stores)
Bouquet handle (obtainable from florists)
White gift or fabric ribbon
Tools (scissors, ruler etc)

These materials are enough to make a medium-sized bouquet.

Try to keep the overall colour of the bouquet's flowers, supporting wires etc white, for the most romantic effect.

TULLE DECORATION

This decoration is used to hide the 'behind' wiring and give a feeling of elegance to the finished bouquet.

Before you start, cut the tulle into squares, the sides of which are the same length as the diameter of the finished bouquet.

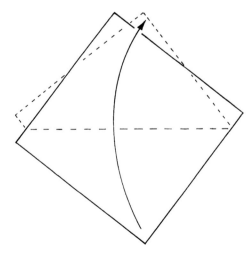

1 Place a square of tulle before you so that it looks like a diamond and fold it in half, off centre, from bottom to top.

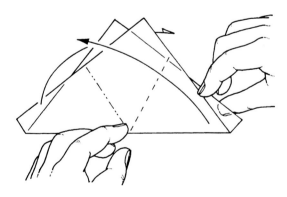

2 From the middle of the bottom, fold the right-hand corner over one-third of the way towards the left. Repeat with the left-hand corner by folding it away from you.

(continued overleaf)

149

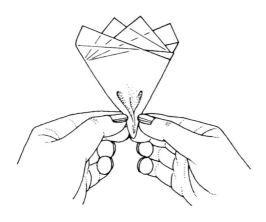

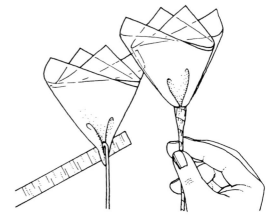

3 Around the bottom point make small, even gathers.

4 Cut a length of 28 gauge wire and bend a small hook into one end. Hook the wire into the gathers. Fasten the gathers, at their base, onto the hooked wire with white tape.

FINISHING OFF
Continue taping to the end of the wire.

For one medium-sized bouquet you will usually need about six or eight tulle decorations.

RIBBON DECORATION

This decoration will give a professional look to any bouquet or corsage. Even though it may look difficult, it is very easy to make if you follow the illustrations carefully. Try to make the decoration out of gift or fabric ribbon matching the colour of the finished bouquet or corsage.

Before you start, cut a length of 30 gauge wire and unwind a little of the ribbon from its spool.

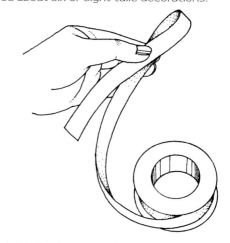

1 With the free end of the ribbon make a fair-sized loop. Try to make the protruding 'tail' longer than the actual loop.

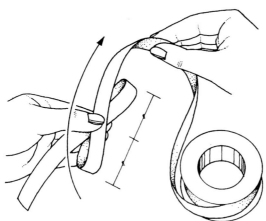

2 From its spool unwind a little more ribbon and bring it up and over the loop you are holding, so making another equal-sized loop. You now should be holding a shape that resembles a figure of eight.

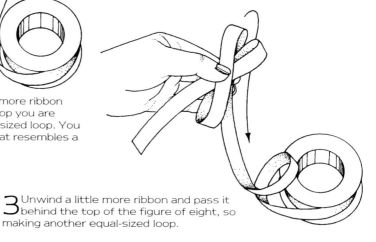

3 Unwind a little more ribbon and pass it behind the top of the figure of eight, so making another equal-sized loop.

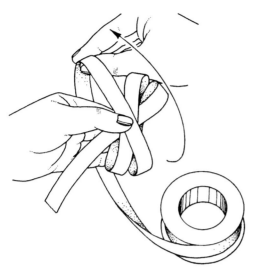

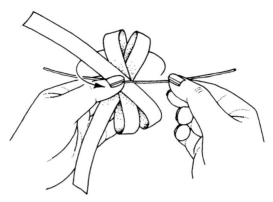

5 Fasten the figures of eight together by twisting the length of 30 gauge wire around their middles.

4 For the final time unwind a little more ribbon. Bring it up and over the figure of eight, so making another equal-sized loop. You should now be holding two slightly crossing figures of eight. Cut the ribbon free from its spool, so making another 'tail' which is the same length as the previous one.

FINISHING OFF
6 Cut V shapes into both the protruding 'tails'.

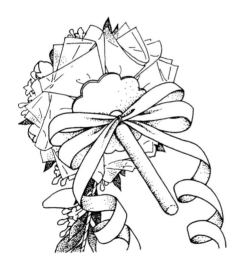

ASSEMBLING THE BRIDAL BOUQUET

Arrange the lilies, bouvardias and trail to suit personal taste and fasten them together with white tape. Place the tulle decorations around the bouquet (hiding the stems) and fasten them into place with a length of white tape. Place all the stems and wires inside the bouquet handle. Otherwise, to make a handle, tightly fasten all the visible stems and wires together with white tape, so completely covering them. Fasten the ribbon decoration around the top of the handle with a length of 28 gauge wire. For a very effective finishing touch make the decoration's 'tails' longer and curl them over the closed blades of a pair of scissors.

MAKING A CORSAGE

For a corsage cut the stems of the required flowers, buds and leaves as short as possible. Arrange the corsage to suit personal taste. Fasten all the stems together with tape of a suitable colour, so completely covering them.

FINISHING OFF
Fasten the ribbon decoration into place with a length of 28 gauge wire.

Arranging Handmade Flowers

Handmade flowers look their best when they are arranged together. There are many methods, techniques and designs for arranging flowers which have developed over the years. In the two styles of arrangement (Western and Oriental) which follow we have tried to help you on the way by giving little pointers. There are no hard and fast rules – flower arranging depends on personal taste and preference.

WESTERN ARRANGEMENT

This style of arrangement is most often triangular in outline and its flowers, buds and leaves are closely packed together, leaving hardly any noticeable space. It is made up of three categories of flowers: main (roses, lilies or any other flower that is strong in personality), accent/colour matching (carnations, freesias and tulips) and supplementary (strawberries, bouvardias and cherry blossoms). In the illustrated example we have used roses (large, medium and small) as the main flowers, carnations as the accent/colour-matching flowers and bouvardias as the supplementary flowers.

Before you start, cut the oasis to fit the required flower container.

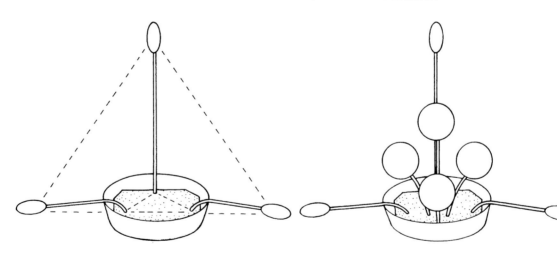

1 Arrange the small flowers into the oasis, so that they are in a triangular figuration. Gently bend the left-hand and right-hand flowers over at right angles to the flower container.

2 Position the main large flowers centrally.

3 Being careful to keep the overall balance of the arrangement, arrange the medium-sized main flowers.

4 Arrange the accent/colour-matching flowers carefully between the main flowers.

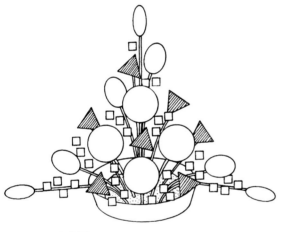

FINISHING OFF
5 Use the supplementary flowers to fill any noticeable spaces.

ORIENTAL ARRANGEMENT

As the art of oriental flower arranging – *Ikebana* – is a very deep and specialised subject, only a very basic outline of the principles involved is given here.

While the Western arrangement requires many flowers, the Oriental arrangement requires just the opposite to make the most visually appealing designs. Try to use flower containers made from black lacquer, hand-thrown pottery or bamboo. You will also need a *kenzan* (spiky flower stand) or a small piece of oasis. Finally, try to find some attractive stones or pebbles.

This style of arrangement is made up of a main branch, with accent flowers and supplementary flowers or leaves. In the illustrated example four branches of forsythia have been used for the main branch. For the accent flowers we have used two camellias, and their leaves and bud have been used as the supplementary item.

Before you start, place the kenzan or oasis in the centre of the chosen container.
(continued overleaf)

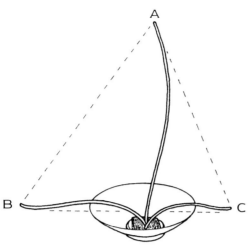

1 Cut one main branch A so that its height is about twice the diameter or height of the flower container (whichever is the greater). Cut another main branch B, so that it is about one-third shorter than branch A. Finally cut another main branch C so that it is about one-third shorter than branch B. Arrange branch A centrally in the kenzan. Next, arrange branch B so that it is at an opposite angle to branch A. Finally, arrange branch C, so that all three branches form the shape of an irregular triangle.

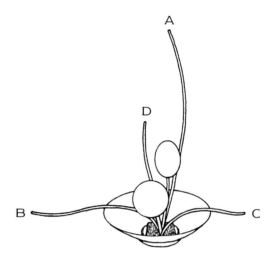

2 Arrange the accent flowers in the centre, so that one is slightly above the other. Cut the remaining forsythia branch D, so that it is about half the height of branch A. Making sure that it supports the main A line, arrange it between branches A and B.

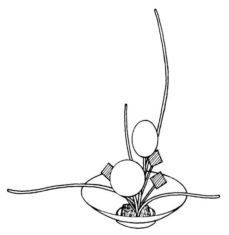

3 To give a feeling of space and harmony arrange the few supplementary items around the accent flowers.

FINISHING OFF
4 Hide the kenzan or oasis by covering it over with the stones or pebbles.

Glossary of Tools and Equipment

Many of the tools required for flower making can be found around the home or in the garage. If you do not have one of the items on the following list, do not be concerned, as it is most likely that you can substitute another in its place. As choice is often a matter of personal preference, please do not stick rigidly to what we have recommended. If you do have a particular tool which you are happy with, then by all means use it. The important thing is that it works for you.

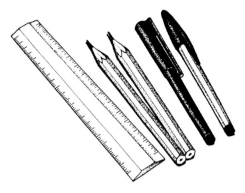

PENS AND PENCILS For tracing out the patterns and drawing around the templates, use a soft pencil (2B).
RULER Needed for measuring paper, fabric and wire.

SCISSORS Have separate pairs for cutting out paper and fabric. The closed scissor blades are used for curling petals.
PLIERS/WIRE CUTTERS For bending and cutting wire. Pliers will also cut wire.

TRACING PAPER If tracing paper is not available, try airmail paper or typing paper.

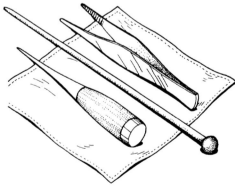

BRADAWL For making small holes in the centre of petals. Alternatively, you can use any other sharp-pointed instrument that you may have at hand.
KNITTING NEEDLE For making tendrils and giving form to the petals (must be round headed).
TWEEZERS Ideal for holding tiny items, like stamens, in place.
COTTON HANDKERCHIEF Used for crinkling technique.

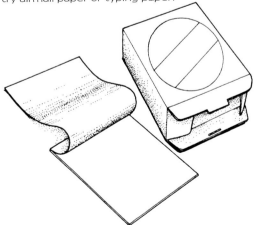

CARD For making stronger templates, try cereal cartons, the backs of notepads and old postcards.

155

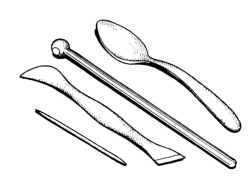

COCKTAIL STICK For placing small amounts of glue along a leaf's spine etc.
SPATULA For scoring the veins of a leaf.
SPOON Useful for shaping petals, and scoring leaf veins.

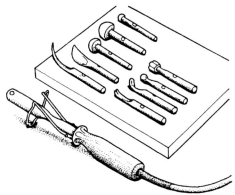

ELECTRIC FLOWER-MAKING IRON
Interchangeable heads used to add softness and texture to petals and leaves. Such an iron is a highly expensive item of equipment to purchase and needs a high level of skill to operate, and may be out of the range of the average craftsperson. However, it is not essential to have one to be able to make the flowers in this book. Obtainable from Hamilworth Floral Products Limited, 23 Lime Road, Dumbarton, Dumbartonshire G82 2RP.

PAPER TISSUES For thickening out stems, especially tulip and bird of paradise.
MIXING BOWL AND MEASURING JUG For dyeing and sizing (use old ones).
NEWSPAPER For covering working surface, except when making a white flower or handling white materials (as these could become soiled with printer's ink). Brown wrapping paper is an alternative.
COTTON WOOL Ideal for making pompons (buds).
RUBBER GLOVES Always wear these to protect hands when dyeing paper or fabric.
CLOTHES PEGS To hang up your dyed or sized material to dry.

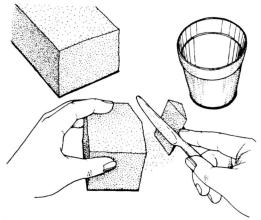

OASIS (florists' foam) For arranging flowers in containers (can be cut to size). Oasis for artificial flowers can be obtained from florists.

SAUCERS AND PAINTBRUSHES For dyeing and sizing. Try to have a separate saucer and paintbrush for each dye.

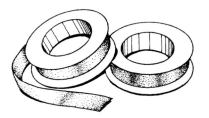

GIFT OR FABRIC RIBBON For decorating corsages and bouquets. Obtainable from stationers, gift shops and haberdashery stores.

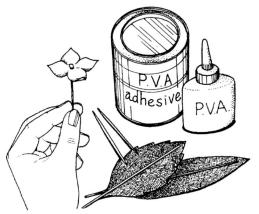

PVA adhesive Safe, ready-mixed white solution adhesive that can be obtained from DIY stores. As it dries hard it is not suitable for gluing together pieces of fabric. Ideal for flower making as it becomes 'invisible' when dry.

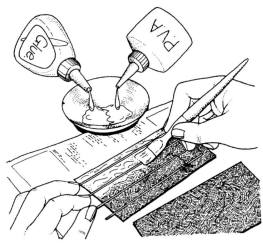

PAPER GLUE Obtainable from stationers. Also try using a 50/50 mixture made up of paper glue and PVA adhesive. As it does not dry hard this is an ideal 'homemade' adhesive for gluing together pieces of fabric.

STICK GLUE Clean, quick and safe glue in a lipstick-type container obtainable from stationers. Ideal for most light paperwork and for gluing on homemade floral tape.

WALLPAPER PASTE Obtainable from DIY stores. Mix together with water as per the instructions on the package. Used for sizing fabric.

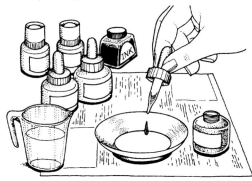

COLOURED INK (not fountain pen ink) Obtainable from art material suppliers. Mix with a little water to control the overall strength of its tint. (Tint is slightly lighter when dry.)

LIQUID PERMEATION SOLUTION Many materials – handmade paper, fabric, silk, etc – contain some kind of starch or waterproofing chemical (even grease or dirty fingermarks) that will prevent any dye from working smoothly. So before you start dyeing use the following solution. Mix two cups of warmish water and two drops of a synthetic detergent (washing-up liquid) together in a bowl. Submerge your material in this solution and let it sit for a few seconds. To finish off, remove the material and tightly squeeze out any excess liquid. This technique is not suitable for crepe paper as the dye will run.

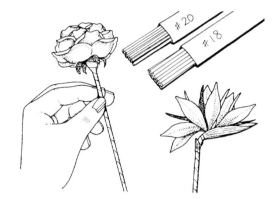

DIRECT DYE Obtainable from art and craft stores. Use hot water to mix, as the temperature will help the dye to work. (Tint is slightly lighter when dry.)

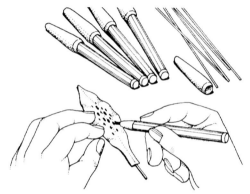

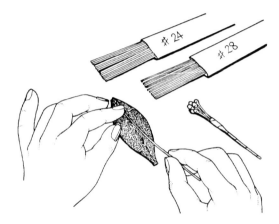

FELT-TIP PENS Obtainable from stationers or art material suppliers. They are useful for flower markings and dyeing white covered wire. Do not use large marker pens.

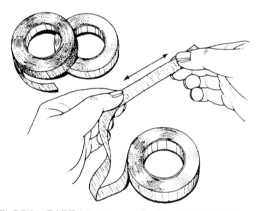

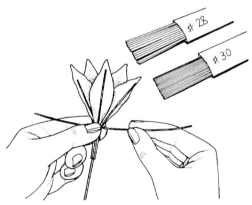

FLORAL TAPE (stem tape/florists' tape/gutta tape) Made from a crepe-like material, impregnated with adhesive. Available in a large range of colours, including several shades of green and brown, and white. It can be dyed to any required colour. Alternatively, you can make your own by cutting a few 1cm (½in) wide strips from a roll of green crepe paper and opening them out into long lengths. Use as normal floral tape but, as you wind it spirally down, fasten it into place using stick glue.

WIRE Obtainable in a large range of thicknesses (gauge), and usually sold in standard lengths. The higher the gauge number, the finer the wire. Wire can be bought covered with paper of a particular colour, or you can cover it with tape.

18 and 20 gauge (plain or green covered wire) are always used for the main stem.

24 and 28 gauge (green covered wire) are used for supporting the back of leaves and in the making of small flower stems.

24 and 28 gauge (white covered wire) are used for supporting the back of petals.

30 gauge is used for any kind of tying work.

INDEX

adhesives
  paper, PVA and stick glue, 157
arrangement, see flower, 21, 152–4

Bird of Paradise and Eucalyptus, 52–7
bouquet
  bridal, 149–51
  flowers for a, 102
  frangipani, 91–2
Bouvardia, 99–102
bowl (mixing), 156, 157
bradawl, 155
brushes, see paint, 156
bud
  description, 7
  making, 20
building up, 17–19

calyx, description, 7
Camellia, 120–3
Canterbury Bell and Forsythia, 34–9
card (paper), 155
Carnation, 48–51
centring technique, 17
Cherry Blossom, 30–3
Clematis, 70–4
clothes pegs, 156
cocktail stick, 156
colouring
  technique, 142–3
  with pen, 158
  with ink, 157
Cosmos, 112–15
cotton, 9
  wool, 156
corsage
  bridal bouquet, 149–51
  frangipani, 91–2
crepe, see paper, 8, 141
crinkling technique, 14
cupping technique, 12, 13
curling technique, 12, 13
cutters, see pliers, 155
Cyclamen, 124, 127

Daffodil, 26–9

decoration
  bow, 150–1
  tulle, 149–50
dye
  application, 140–3
  source, 157, 158

embossing technique, see leaf, 11
Eucalyptus, see Bird of Paradise, 52–7
  Nerine, arranged with, 119

felt-tip, see pens, 155, 158
finishing technique, 21
floral tape, see tape, 158
flowers
  parts, description, 7

arrangement
  Western, 152, 153
  Oriental, 153, 154
  single vase, 21
fluting technique, 13
foam (florists'), see oasis, 156
Forsythia, see Canterbury Bell, 34–9
Foxglove, 66–9
Frangipani, 89–93
Freesia, 44–7
frilling technique, 13

gift ribbon, see ribbon, 9, 156
Gladiolus, 103–7
glue, see adhesives, 157
gradation technique, 141, 143

INDEX

handkerchief, 14, 155
heating technique, see iron, 12, 156
Hydrangea, 62–5

ink, see colouring, 157
Iris, 58–61
iron, application, 12, 156

jug (measuring), 156

knitting needle, see needle, 155

leaves
    description, 7
    embossing, 11
Lily, 94–8
liquid permeation solution, 157

measuring
    length, 155
    metric and imperial, 9
    volume, 156
mixing, see bowl, 156, 157

needle
    and cotton, 78
    knitting, 155
Nerine, 116–19

oasis (foam), 156

paint, see colouring, 142–3, 157
    brushes, 156

paper
    crepe, 8, 141
    handmade, 6, 8
    newspaper, 156
    tissues, 156
    tracing, 155
    wrapping, 156
paste, see adhesives, 157
pegs, see clothes, 156
pencils, 155
pens, felt-tip, ball point
    application, 155
    source, 158
Peony, 133–9
petals
    description, 7
    cutting out, 145–8
Petunia, 84–8
pistils, discretion, 7
pliers, 155
poplin, 9
Poppy, 108–11
pot (flower), 25, 124
PVA, see adhesives, 157

ribbon (gift or fabric)
    application, 9
    source, 156
Rose, 128–32
    see also curling, 12, 13

ruler, 155

Salvia, 80–3
satin, 9
saucers, 156
scissors, 155
silk, 9
sizing technique, 144
Snowdrop, 22–5
spatula, 156
spoon, 156
stamens
    description, 7
    source, 9
    application, 140
stem, description, 7
Strawberry, 75–9
stretching technique, 13

tape
    source, 9, 158
    preparation, 140
template, making a, 10
tissues, see paper, 156
tendril, making a, 102
trumpet shape, making a, 27–9
Tulip, 40–3
tweezers, 155

velvet, 9

wire
    source, 9
    application, 158
    cutters, see pliers, 155
    technique, 15, 16
wool, see cotton, 156